UNFOLDING TIME

*This eight publication in the series*
*"Collected Writings of the Orpheus Institute"*
*is edited by Darla Crispin*

# UNFOLDING TIME

Studies in Temporality in
Twentieth-Century Music

*Mark Delaere*

*Justin London*

*Pascal Decroupet*

*Bruce Brubaker*

*Ian Pace*

COLLECTED WRITINGS OF THE

O R P H E U S
INSTITUTE

Leuven University Press

2009

# CONTENTS

# PREFACE

It is not surprising that the landscape of musical scholarship in the early twenty-first century should reflect aspects of 'unfinished business' from the twentieth. Perhaps nowhere is this more apparent than in approaches to musical temporality.

Temporality, as an issue for composers and musical theorists, was not only brought to the fore but also problematised during the twentieth century. 'How time passes' became one of the key issues confronting music in the Modernist age even before its reification in the title of Karlheinz Stockhausen's iconic essay of 1957[1]. The question took many forms — from how music might reinvent a capacity for extended utterance when bereft of the dynamising forces of functional tonality to how non-linear concepts of time may be accommodated within music which, whatever the composer's aspirations, is bound in performance to the sequential linearity of beginning, continuing and ending.

Initially, the terrain for these debates was essentially that of the musical work and its associated theoretical constructs. When Igor Stravinsky, in his Charles Elliot Norton lectures, *Poetics of Music*[2] (1939–1940) differentiated between ontological and psychological time, he was concerned with these concepts as they are encoded in types of composition, rather than experienced in performance — other than insofar as the latter may arise as a secondary consequence of the former. However, as the century drew to a close, a general shift of focus towards performance meant that questions of temporality also turned in this direction.

Alongside issues of how time is conceived, structured and manipulated within a composition, there arose parallel considerations of

---

1. Stockhausen, Karlheinz. 1963b. "... wie die Zeit vergeht ...". In his "Texte zur Musik", vol. I, pp. 99–139. Cologne: Verlag M. DuMont Schauberg. Revised and annotated version of the text first published in "Die Reihe" 3 (1957): 13–42. Translation by Cornelius Cardew, as "... How Time Passes ..." in the English edition of "Die Reihe" 3 (1959): 10–40.
2. Igor Stravinsky, *Poetics of Music, in the form of six lessons,* (Cambridge, Mass.: Harvard University Press), 1970), pp. 39–43.

how it is perceived within the sonorous unfolding of a performance. In particular, cases where what is written and what is heard are widely at variance came increasingly to be viewed from a perspective which saw these two elements as of equal importance. Instead of text taking precedence, thanks to its capacity to sustain a impressive superstructure of conceptual complexity, intellectual fashion began to swing to the not unreasonable, but hitherto muted, view that, in music, the sounds that strike the ear during a performance are, if anything, of greater relevance than the patterns that assail the eye when examining a score or the concepts that flood the mind when one reads an analysis.

This trend was already well under way before the millennium. Thus, in 1971, the composer Iannis Xenakis could write in his 'Formalised Music' that '*Linear polyphony destroys itself by its very complexity; what one hears is in reality nothing but a mass of notes in various registers*' (significantly, it is the self-defeating, futile complexity of linear polyphony, and not some inadequacy of the hearing faculty, which is seen to be at fault in this impasse)[3]. Nevertheless, the focus upon musical time as it is *experienced*, rather than *conceived*, has been given added impetus in recent years with the emergence in music and the other arts of the phenomenon of practice-based research. This approach, which places the artist's practice at the focal centre of its scrutiny, has had the dual effect of encouraging composers to re-connect with the performed identity of their compositions and of enfranchising performers and their *métier* within debates as to the essential nature of music.

Appropriately, then, this volume is a compilation of post-millennial musings on music and time which brings together a range of approaches, both methodologically and stylistically, and which embodies the principle that composers, music theorists and performers have much to gain from mutual exchange of ideas and experience concerning the artform with which they are all variously engaged. This is a principle that lies at the heart of the work of the Orpheus Institute and informs its full range of activities — postgraduate education programmes, seminars and research.

---

3. Iannis Xenakis, *Formalized Music*, translation by Christopher Butchers, G. H. Hopkins, John Challifour, (Bloomington, University Press, 1971), p. 5.

Every year, the Orpheus Institute holds its International Orpheus Academy for Music & Theory. In 2007, the Academy, brought together not only music theoreticians and analysts but also performers and composers to debate the subject of music and time within a research environment that focused specifically upon questions concerning musical creation, as part of the wider discourse on 'research in-and-through musical practice'. **Unfolding Time: Studies in Temporality in Twentieth-Century Music** collates and records the contributions of the principal figures from the 2007 Academy: Bruce Brubaker (New England Conservatory, Boston, MASS.), Pascal Decroupet (Université de Nice — Sophia Antipolis), Mark Delaere (University of Leuven), Justin London (Carleton College, MN), and Ian Pace (Dartington College of Arts).

Reflecting the eclectic nature of this gathering of individuals, **Unfolding Time** does not display a uniformly 'traditional' approach to music analysis. While the reader will find some closely-argued analytical studies within these pages, s/he will also be confronted with questions concerning cognition, aesthetics and musical performance, as well as an experimental text that harks back to the writings of John Cage. In reconsidering many of the tropes concerning time that so captivated thinkers of the twentieth century, the contributors to this volume offer a selection of contemporary approaches to temporality, and an articulation of its relationship both to our twenty-first century cultural landscape in general and to the developing field of artistic research in particular.

\* \* \*

In 'Tempo, Metre, Rhythm: Time in Twentieth-Century Music', Mark Delaere opens the discourse by providing an overview of post-millennial scholarship on music and time, which he interrogates through more specific discussion of repertoire by Arnold Schoenberg, Olivier Messiaen and others. He uses this as a means of uncovering the many and complex problems that confront composers, who must come to terms with an ever-expanding array of tools for the elucidation of rhythm, metre and tempo, some of which have enabled transcendence of purely schematic representations of time in music. He does caution us, however, that the evolution of notation demands from us a correspondingly evolving awareness of its impact upon performers, and of the tension between the composer's sense of music's 'wholeness' and the performer's necessarily heightened sense of music as temporally ephemeral.

This aspect of Delaere's discussion leads into the second contribution, Justin London's 'Temporal Complexity in Modern and Post-Modern Music: A critique from Cognitive Aesthetics'. London places the experiential aspect of temporal perception at the core of his argument, so that the first-person aural experience of the music is his primary concern. Through a review of portions of the psychological literature on perception and cognition, linked with close readings of works by Olivier Messiaen and Milton Babbitt, London guides the reader toward an understanding of the distinction between artistic and aesthetic properties, which leads him to an evaluation of the relationship between rhythmic complexity and aesthetic value. This final argument provides one helpful approach to the many paradoxes surrounding musical temporality.

Discussions of music and time may focus in upon the infinitesimally small, or speculate about the infinitely vast. The two studies that follow London's analysis illustrate this dichotomy, and various attempts to bridge it, very well. In 'Rhythms — durations — rhythmic cells — groups: Concepts of micro level time organisation in serial music and their consequences on shaping time on higher structural levels', Pascal Decroupet assembles close readings of works by Igor Stravinsky, Olivier Messiaen, Pierre Boulez and Karlheinz Stockhausen to explore how temporal characteristics at the micro level leave their imprint upon the experience of musical time and, in particular, how these composers concentrated upon this aspect of creation as being an important source of innovation. Decroupet's analytical approaches open up another of the paradoxes relating to musical time, the inextricable relationship between the *apparent* restrictions of serial composition (particularly in the extreme manner of Boulez and Stockhausen), and their actual promise of a form of 'subjective freedom' *within* serial music.

In considering the question of 'freedom' in relation to twentieth-century music, it would be impossible to overlook the philosophy-in-practice of one of its most influential thinkers, John Cage. In 'Time is Time: Temporal Signification in Music', Bruce Brubaker presents a written text both as a Cage tribute and a Cage critique, confronting the reader once again with the provocative empty spaces of Cage's challenge to the musical world of the twentieth century. Brubaker's discussion is both a 'timely' reminder of the apparently inexhaustible, questioning energy that emerges from Cage's lifelong project, and an artwork in itself. Like Cage, Brubaker resists closure and conclusion, leaving an open space, literally and metaphorically, as the cue for the final article.

Ian Pace's extensive discussion on 'Notation, Time and the Performer's Relationship to the Score in Contemporary Music', points up an important issue for those immersed in questions of musical practice: the performer lives permanently with an encoded sense of the subjective narrative construction of Western music history. This narrative creates a background in which performers must make a vast array of decisions. Pace proposes that performers may deal with this potentially overwhelming problem by working 'against the grain' of positivistic views of the score. Through his descriptions of this approach within the article, he opens up a set of performative options that have a special appeal to performers of modern and post-modern music. Re-presenting works by Elliott Carter, Mauricio Kagel, Pierre Boulez, Morton Feldman, Karlheinz Stockhausen and others, Pace offers to music analysis a Lacanian way of 'looking awry' at its own arguments. Meanwhile, he opens up possibilities to music performance that fuse performative practicality with an uncompromising aim for a specific set of aesthetic ideals.

\* \* \*

Ultimately, the articles within this volume form part of a wider, inclusive dialogue in which theory and practice link together for their mutual betterment. As already stated, this is one of the key tenets of the Orpheus Institute, articulated though its programmes, its annual Academies and its newly-formed Orpheus Research Centre in Music (ORCiM). It is hoped that **Unfolding Time** supplies a positive early diagnosis concerning the youthful field of artistic research, and holds out the promise that this field may evolve and expand to enrich musical understanding for years to come.

*Darla Crispin*

# TEMPO, METRE, RHYTHM. TIME IN TWENTIETH-CENTURY MUSIC MUSIC

*Mark Delaere**

---

One of the many paradoxes in the life of a music scholar is that music is said to be the quintessential *temporal* art form, whereas the far greater portion of the theoretical and analytical literature on art music deals with *pitch* independently of temporal factors. Curricula in conservatories of music and university music departments have subjects such as harmony, counterpoint and ear training, with a focus on pitch intervals and chords, but it is hard to find a course on tempo, metre and rhythm. The roots of this disparity go back at least to the eighteenth century. Jean-Philippe Rameau's and Hugo Riemann's writings on tonality are landmarks in the history of music theory, while throughout the nineteenth and twentieth centuries, most music textbooks dealt with harmony and counterpoint. Powerful analytical systems such as Schenkerian analysis and pitch-class set theory were developed during the twentieth century to reveal the underlying structural principles of pitch organization. But until recently, independent studies of musical time of comparable scope and depth were underrepresented. Only from the nineteenth century onwards have isolated theoretical studies of musical time seen the light, first as spin-offs from philosophical reflection[1] or as the result of historical and analytical research[2]. Other methodological approaches to the study of musical time, within the fields of music psychology[3]

---

* I am grateful to Maarten Quanten, Klaas Coulembier and Jochem Valkenburg for reading an earlier draft of this article and for their helpful comments. My gratitude also goes to Kathryn Bailey Puffett and Darla Crispin for the informed comments and for the stylistic finetuning of this text.

---

1. See Moritz Hauptmann, *Die Natur der Harmonik und Metrik*, Leipzig 1853.
2. See Hugo Riemann, *System der musikalischen Metrik und Rhythmik*, Leipzig 1903.
3. For an early example of the extension of Carl Stumpf's 'Tonpsychologie' to the domain of rhythm see Kurt Koffka, 'Experimental-Untersuchung zur Lehre vom Rhythmus', in: *Zeitschrift für Psychologie* 44 (1909).

and musical aesthetics, have since been gradually, and initially hesitantly, added to this corpus of writing [4].

A lack of attention to the rhythmic structure of music can have disastrous consequences, as will be shown by a short analytical discussion of the final bar of Arnold Schoenberg's Op. 19/6 (1911) (reproduced in its entirety in Example 1).

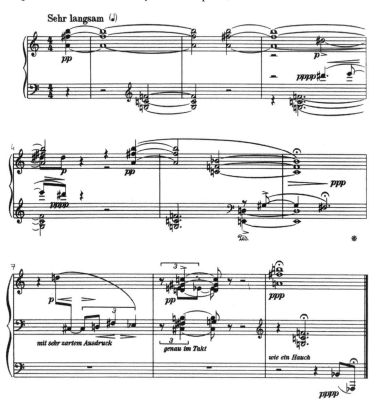

*Example 1. A. Schoenberg, Sechs kleine Klavierstücke, Op. 19/6*
© *Universal Edition, Vienna.*

Whereas a beat pattern and metre can barely be defined during the first six bars of the piece, the formal design of these bars is crystal

---

4. An authoritative example is Gisèle Brelet, *Le temps musical*, Paris 1949, which will be briefly discussed further on.

clear. Bb. 1–6 are obviously constructed as a musical sentence, with the model presented in bb. 1–2, its varied repetition in bb. 2–4, and a continuation in bb. 5 (with upbeat)–6. According to Erwin Ratz, the basic function of the continuation phase of a musical sentence is:

> …that some of the motives presented in the two-bar unit are dropped, so as to achieve a condensation and acceleration of the musical flow. As a general rule, the developmental [or continuation] phase implies a harmonic acceleration as well[5].

Similarly, according to William Caplin:

> The formal function of continuation has two outstanding characteristics: fragmentation, a reduction in the size of units; and harmonic acceleration, an increase in the rate of harmonic change.
> A third main feature of continuation function (…) is harmonic sequence[6].

The harmonic acceleration of the continuation phase in comparison to the model and its varied repetition is obvious: it is provoked by the anticipated repetition of the lower trichord *G–C–F* and its twofold sequence *C–F–Bb*; *E–D* (framing interval only). In contrast, the upper trichord is dropped after its initial repetition, giving way to the condensation and acceleration of the lower trichord.

---

5. See Erwin Ratz, *Einführung in die musikalische Formenlehre*, 3rd edition, Vienna 1973, pp. 21–22: '…dass ein Teil der im Zweitakter exponierten Motive fallen gelassen und so eine Verdichtung und Beschleunigung der musikalischen Darstellung erzielt wird. In der Regel findet im Entwicklungsteil auch eine Beschleunigung in der harmonischen Disposition statt' (all translations in this chapter are mine unless indicated otherwise). Ratz's book is the single best primary source for an adequate understanding of Schoenberg's analytical method. For an attempt to apply principles of Schoenberg, the analyst of tonal music, to Schoenberg, the composer of atonal music, see my *Funktionelle Atonalität. Analytische Strategien für die frei-atonale Musik der Wiener Schule* (Veröffentlichungen zur Musikforschung 14), Wilhelmshaven 1993, which includes a more extensive discussion of Op. 19/6 on pp. 80–84. For the single best secondary source and the development of Schoenberg's analytical approach into a self-sufficient music theory, see William B. Caplin, *Classical Form: a Theory of Formal Functions for the Instrumental Music of Haydn, Mozart and Beethoven*, New York 1998.
6. See Caplin, *Classical Form*, p. 10 and p. 260 (footnote 6).

The sentence is followed by a short contrasting section (bb. 7–8) and a 'repetition' (b. 9). The key question as to what is being repeated in b. 9 is invariably answered in the analytical literature on the subject by referring to the beginning of the piece, with the addition of two extra pitches. In this literature, which is very extensive, one may read the wildest speculations on the presence of these two final pitches of the piece (*Bb–Ab*), none of them entirely satisfactory or convincing[7]. Taking the rhythmic structure into consideration, it is clear that it is not the beginning of the piece which is being repeated in the final bar, but the continuation phase of the sentence, thus:

– In b. 5, the upper pitches of the trichords are *B–F–Bb–G#*, with IOI 1-2-1
– In b. 9, the upper pitches of the (partly elliptic) trichords are *B–F–Bb–Ab*, with IOI 1-2-1 (contracted)[8]

This brief analytical example demonstrates that taking temporal aspects into account is not only beneficial for the study of the rhythmic structure of a piece but can also be helpful in elucidating unresolved problems in the analysis of its pitch structure.

It is most fortunate in this respect that a growing interest in the study of musical time can be observed during the last ten years, following some pioneering work in the 1960s–1980s[9]. This enhanced interest was set off by one of the most influential publications in this field and a source of inspiration to this day. In his *The Time of Music*, Jonathan Kramer developed an awareness of

---

7. The online bibliography of the Arnold Schoenberg Centre in Vienna lists more than forty publications on op. 19. In their widely used *Music Analysis in Theory and Practice*, London 1988, Jonathan Dunsby and Arnold Whittal demonstrate no less than five different analytical approaches to Schoenberg's op. 19/6.
8. The Inter Onset Interval (IOI) indicates the timespan between the attack points of successive events. In this case the IOI is expressed in crotchets. The IOI of the two trichords at the beginning of the piece (b. 1) is 3 crotchets.
9. I just mention Grosvenor Cooper and Leonard B. Meyer, *The Rhythmic Structure of Music*, Chicago 1960; Edward T. Cone, *Musical Form and Musical Performance*, New York 1968; and Fred Lerdahl and Ray Jackendoff, *A Generative Theory of Tonal Music*, Cambridge 1983.

the non-linearity and multiplicity of musical time. Since the appearance of this seminal work, David Epstein has documented empirical research on brain functions during the performance of music, thereby closing the gap between music theory concerning musical time, cognitive studies and performance practice. Christopher Hasty has introduced a more differentiated approach to the categories metre and rhythm, previously described respectively as 'rigid pattern' and 'flexible phenomenon'. Finally, an elegant combination of music theoretical and psychological research has been offered by Justin London [10].

With the exception of Kramer and, to a certain extent, Hasty, a searching inquiry of contemporary music is lacking in most of these studies and others like them. Two explanations are put forward for this neglect: either the theoretical models concerning musical time are considered to be universally valid — the subcutaneous regulative reasoning behind this assertion being that if contemporary music fails to meet the criteria of the model, it fails to be (valuable) music — or they are regarded as unable to cope with the intricate rhythms typical of twentieth-century music. It goes without saying that these explanations are mutually exclusive. Consequently, it is just about time (if this phrasing is allowed) that a book such as this one on the organization of musical time in contemporary music sees the light. In this introductory chapter, I will discuss significant developments in how compositions deal with time since 1900, with an emphasis on music before 1950 so as to provide a historical point of reference for the following chapters on music from the second half of the twentieth century. However, I should emphasize that this essay should by no means be construed as a comprehensive survey of these developments, something which is clearly impossible within its limited scope. Instead I would like to sketch out with selected examples some of the most profound changes that occurred in the thinking of musical time

---

10. Jonathan Kramer, *The Time of Music. New Meanings, New Temporalities, New Listening Strategies*, New York 1988; David Epstein, *Shaping Time. Music, the Brain, and Performance*, New York 1997; Christopher Hasty, *Meter as Rhythm*, New York 1997; Justin London, *Hearing in Time. Psychological Aspects of Musical Meter*, New York 2004.

during the previous century. The terminological discussion preceding this overview is conceived in a similarly introductory manner [11].

Terminological issues on time in twentieth-century music benefit from a distinction between three levels of identification in activities such as score reading (grouping of events) and listening to music (perception of groupings). Categories of musical time are operational at either the surface, intermediary or background level. Contrary to what the use of these Schenkerian concepts might suggest, there are no implications of hierarchy among the three levels of identification. Neither are the categories of musical time fixed to any of these levels of identification. Beat or tempo, for instance, can operate on the surface, the intermediary or the background level, depending on context. With the exception of the last three terms defined, the terminology described below is applicable to music before 1950.

**Rhythm** can be defined as a succession of at least two equal or non-equal proportional durations.

A **beat** is a mechanical succession of equal proportional durations. Beat is related to tempo (MM, 'bpm': beats per minute) and meter (denominator). Its level of identification is conditioned by the rhythmic structure in which it appears (or not).

**Metre** consists of a grouping of a number of beats; metre can express a hierarchy between beats ('downbeat', 'metric accent').

**Tempo** links beat to clock time; tempo defines the speed of musical events, but not their proportions.

A **pulse** is created as soon as a regular pattern of equal durations appears. This can be the case with a beat as well, but pulses are generally faster than beats and always at the surface (or intermediary) level.

A **basic pulse** results from the grouping of pulses, which can be different from the notated beat, meter and tempo. Example 2 clarifies most of the concepts defined until now.

---

11. The definitions presented below were drafted by Klaas Coulembier and Maarten Quanten in the context of a research project on tempo relations in contemporary music directed by me at the Musicology department of the University of Leuven. Some of these definitions are slightly different from received wisdom. This was unavoidable in view of the temporal phenomena encountered in (some) contemporary music.

*Example 2.*

**Absolute tempo** is the speed of a periodic pulse. In a succession of semiquavers at crotchet = 60, the semiquaver note has an absolute tempo of 240 bpm.

An **anti-metric figure** is a rhythmic pattern which disturbs the beat. In a 4/4 metre, a triplet of crotchets is an anti-metric figure, whereas a triplet of quavers — being a subdivision instead of a disturbance of the beat — is not.

**Polyrhythm** is created by the presence of two or more different pulses within the beat (or within the basic pulse). The superposition of different subdivisions of the beat is a common phenomenon in all polyphonic music. Admittedly, this is a very broad definition of polyrhythm. As a matter of fact, the concept of polyrhythm is restricted most of the time to combined rhythmic structures that are more or less incongruent. Some authors accept only periodicities with non-integer multiples as polyrhythmic[12].

**Polymetre** can be defined as the presence of either two or more different groupings of the beat — as in, for instance, the superposition of a 2/4- and a 3/4-metre —, or of two or more different basic pulses that are reducible to a common beat — as in, for instance, the superposition of a 6/8- and a 4/4-metre. Depending on the arithmetic relationship between the combined metres, polymetre can create short- or long-span cyclic periodicities.

---

12. See for instance London, *Hearing in Time*, p. 49.

In **Polytempo** two or more different beats expressed by different metronome markings are present; the beats are not reducible to a common beat. It should be noted that a strict delineation of poly-metre and polytempo is impossible, and even undesirable. The difference is only gradual and is related to the degree of cyclicity, i.e. the frequency of points of coincidence between tempi. A superposition of a crotchet = 90 and a crotchet = 60 is likely to be perceived as polymetre, whereas the superposition of crotchet = 120 and crotchet = 121 is not.

**Irrational metre** is a metre the denominator of which is not an exponent of 2 (x2, x4, x8, x16, etc.). One could describe irrational metre as the 'metricization' of the anti-metric figure. For instance, a 6/7 irrational metre has six pulses of a septuplet.

In spite of its name the concept of **metric modulation** has more to do with tempo (relations) than with metre. Metric modulation is a proportional change in tempo, based on a 'common pulse' between the consecutive tempi. This technique facilitates the exact performance of frequent and apparently complex tempo changes. A succession of the tempi 100 and 133.33 bpm may seem difficult and unperformable at first, but on hindsight discloses itself as a mere transition from a dotted quaver to a crotchet as the beat or pulse. The concept of metric modulation thus applies to a succession of tempi. The superposition of different but related tempo layers shares the same concern for structural coherence of tempi as metric modulation, but it lacks the transitional characteristic of a 'modulation'. The technique of metric modulation was put into practice for both local and large-scale structural and formal purposes.

**Large-scale polyrhythm**, also known as long-range or structural polyrhythm, is a combination of two or more basic pulses at the background level. Large-scale polyrhythm is independent of the referential beat, tempo or metre, and it moves at an (extremely) slow pace. The technique is put into practice at the pre-compositional stage, since in many cases composers use large-scale polyrhythms to structure their work beforehand (i.e. before the actual process of composition).

I have selected six topics that are of paramount importance for the dramatic changes in thinking and imagining musical time since 1900. The first paradigmatic shift is the EMANCIPATION OF RHYTHM in Western art music. Disregarding isorhythmic procedures in fourteenth-century music, time was organized independently from pitch for the first time at the beginning of the twentieth century. Instead of serving as a mere articulation of pitch structures, as in Classical-Romantic music[13], rhythm can act as the principal structural and formal force of a composition. The possibility of an autonomous rhythmic organization was demonstrated in a brilliant way in Olivier Messiaen's analysis of rhythmic cells in Igor Stravinsky's *Rite of Spring* (1911–1913) (see Example 3).

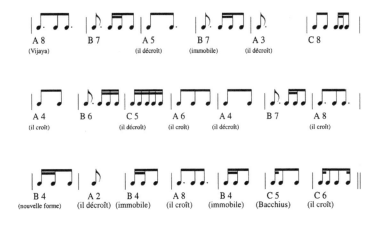

*Example 3. O. Messiaen's analysis of the beginning (rehearsal numbers 142 to 148) of the* Sacrificial Dance, *quoted from his* Traité de rythme, de couleur, et d'ornithologie, *vol. 2, Paris 1995, pp. 130 and beginning of the* Sacrificial Dance *with indication of the rhythmic cells.*

Messiaen identifies three alternating rhythmic cells A, B and C. Each repetition brings a variation of the duration: A shrinks at first from 8 (semiquavers) to 5 and 3, and grows thereafter to 4 and 6; B is stable at first, but shrinks afterwards to 6; and C is shrinking

---

13. 'Harmonic rhythm' is a significant term in this respect. It indicates the speed of chord changes, but this speed is governed by a harmonic (tonal) instead of a rhythmic logic.

*Example 3.*

from 8 to 5. These 'personnages rythmiques' act and behave like rhythmic characters on a stage. They are the driving force in the musical narrative to which the presentation and development of themes or motives, or the harmonic organization is of secondary importance only. Criticism can be raised to some details of Messiaen's analysis—his disregarding of the fermata in the first A cell, or the 'downbeat' function of the double bass octaves—but not to its basic assumptions. *The Rite of Spring* is arguably one of the most influential compositions of the twentieth century, whose importance as a model is comparable to that of Ludwig van Beethoven's Symphony No. 5 op. 67 (1808) to the nineteenth century. Its autonomous rhythmic organization emboldened Messiaen and other post-war composers to invent music in which time is an independent and central parameter[14].

Another important development in the composition of time since 1900 is the EXPANSION OF MUSICAL METRE. Asymmetric or non-isochronous metres emanated from (Eastern European) folk music and jazz. They had been applied sporadically from the mid-nineteenth century onwards by composers such as Modest Mussorgsky and Antonín Dvořák, but the extensive use of asymmetric metre in Western art music dates from the first half of the twentieth century. Béla Bartók and once again Stravinsky are to be cited in this context. Example 4 shows a famous specimen: the beginning of the *Scherzo* from Bartók's *String Quartet no. 5* (1934), in which the 9/8 metre has three non-isochronous beats: 4+2+3 ('Alla bulgarese' or 'aksak' rhythm).

In the 9/8 opening movement of the same composer's *Sonata for Two Pianos and Percussion* (1937) the rhythmic structures are both simultaneously and successively organized as 3+3+3; 2+2+2+3; 3+2+2+2; 4+2+3; 3+2+4 etc.

In twentieth-century music the metrical framework is further expanded by frequent changes of metre, substantial syncopations and unexpected rhythmic accents; techniques that undermine periodicity and predictability and, as a result, allow for compositions in which rhythmic development is the driving force. Frequent changes of metre may result from so-called additive

---

14. For more information on Messiaen's *Rite of Spring* analysis and its impact on Pierre Boulez, Karel Goeyvaerts and Karlheinz Stockhausen, see my 'Olivier Messiaen's Analysis Seminar and the Development of Post-War Serial Music', in: *Music Analysis* 21/1 (2002), pp. 35–51.

*Example 4. B. Bartók,* Scherzo *from String quartet no. 5, bb. 1–10*
© *Universal Edition, Vienna.*

metre in which (generally fast) beats or pulses are grouped in
metres according to rhythmic context. One could say that in this
case, metre results from rhythm instead of the other way around.
But even within a symmetric and stable metre an attenuation or
even annihilation of metric accent and beat may be observed. This
can occur even in twentieth-century music not primarily reputed
for its rhythmic innovation, as can be illustrated by a quotation
from Alban Berg about the absence of a periodic beat at the sur-

face level of Schoenberg's music. According to Berg, rhythmic differentiation is one of the reasons why Schoenberg's music is so difficult to understand:

> To feel the beauty of such themes (and of his music in general) with the heart [...] requires the hearing faculty of an ear that is set the most difficult task with regard to rhythm, which—here and everywhere in Schoenberg's music—rises to a hitherto unheard-of pitch of variety and differentiation [...]. One would either have to be very deaf or very malicious to describe a music that manifests such richness of rhythms (and in such a concentrated form both successively and simultaneously) as 'arhythmic' [15].

However, the most radical innovation in the composition of time in twentieth-century music is arguably the use of (non-metric) ABSOLUTE RHYTHM. To imagine rhythmic structures independently from metre is to deviate considerably from common practice in the composition of Western art music. With absolute rhythm, durations do not result from the division of a metrical pattern or beat but are used as values *per se*. In the Preface to the score of his *Quatuor pour la Fin du Temps* (1941) Messiaen expounds how a short duration (e.g. a semiquaver) and its multiplications may be substituted for 'beat' and 'metre' as the composer's point of departure. Figure 1 shows an excerpt from this Preface, the 'Petite théorie de mon langage rythmique' in which three rhythmic forms are described [16]. Both the added value ('valeur ajoutée') and the augmented and diminished rhythms ('rythmes augmentés ou diminués') are very effective in making a regular beat or metre impossible. Barlines are used by Messiaen as a graphic help or as a point of orientation for performers only; they do not have a musical function. The third rhythmic form presented in Figure 1 is the use of non-retrogradable rhythms ('rythmes non-rétrogradables'), showing Messiaen's predilection for symmetrical orderings—

---

15. Alban Berg, 'Why is Schoenberg's Music so Difficult to Understand?' (1924) (transl. by C. Cardew), London 1965, p. 195.
16. Olivier Messiaen's *Technique de mon langage musical*, Paris 1944, and, especially, his *Traité de rythme, de couleur, et d'ornithologie*, Paris 1994-2002 deal more extensively with his rhythmic theory and practice, but the concise presentation in the Preface to the *Quatuor* serves the purpose of this introductory chapter perfectly well.

## II. - Petite théorie de mon langage rythmique.

J'emploie ici, comme dans la plupart de mes ouvrages, un langage rythmique spécial. En plus d'une secrète prédilection pour les nombres premiers (5, 7, 11, etc.), les notions de "mesure" et de "temps" y sont remplacées par le sentiment d'une valeur brève (la double croche, par exemple) et de ses multiplications libres; et aussi par certaines "formes rythmiques", qui sont : la valeur ajoutée; les rythmes augmentés ou diminués; les rythmes non rétrogradables; la pédale rythmique.

a) **La valeur ajoutée.** Valeur brève, ajoutée à un rythme quelconque, soit par une note, soit par un silence, soit par le point.

Par une note :

Par un silence :

Par le point :

Ordinairement, et comme dans les exemples ci-dessus, le rythme est presque toujours immédiatement pourvu de la valeur ajoutée, sans avoir été entendu au préalable à l'état simple.

b) **Les rythmes augmentés ou diminués.** Un rythme peut être immédiatement suivi de son augmentation ou diminution, suivant diverses formes; en voici quelques exemples (dans chacun d'eux, la 1ʳᵉ mesure contient le rythme normal, la 2ᵉ mesure son augmentation ou diminution) :

Ajout du tiers des valeurs :

Retrait du quart des valeurs :

Ajout du point :

Retrait du point :

Augmentation classique :

Diminution classique :

Ajout du double des valeurs :

Retrait des 2/3 des valeurs :

Ajout du triple des valeurs :

Retrait des 3/4 des valeurs :

On peut user aussi d'augmentations et diminutions inexactes.

*Figure 1. O. Messiaen, Petite théorie de mon langage musical. Excerpt from the Preface to* Quatuor pour la Fin du Temps.

Exemple :

Ce rythme contient 3 croches (diminution classique des 3 noires), plus le point (valeur ajoutée), qui rend la diminution inexacte.

c) **Les rythmes non rétrogradables.** Qu'on les lise de droite à gauche ou de gauche à droite, l'ordre de leurs valeurs reste le même. Cette particularité existe dans tous les rythmes divisibles en 2 groupes rétrogradés l'un par rapport à l'autre, avec valeur centrale "commune".

Exemple :

Succession de rythmes non rétrogradables (chaque mesure contenant un de ces rythmes) :

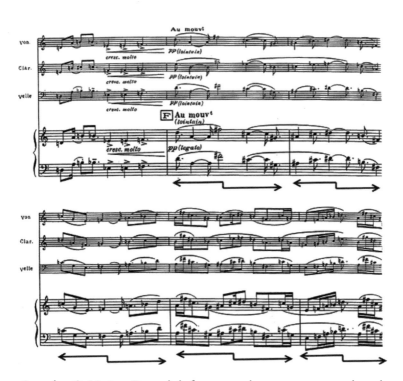

*Example 5. O. Messiaen,* Danse de la fureur, pour les sept trompettes, *rehearsal letter F (from* Quatuor pour la Fin du Temps*) © Editions Durand, Paris.*

27

the equivalent in the rhythmic domain of the 'modes à transpositions limitées' in the domain of pitch.

Example 5 shows a passage from the unisono movement of the *Quatuor*. From rehearsal letter F onwards each 'bar' contains a non-retrogradable rhythm.

In addition to the emancipation of rhythm, expansion of metre and absolute (non-metric) rhythm, the emergence of the concept of MULTIDIMENSIONAL AND NON-LINEAR MUSICAL TIME is one of the topics to be discussed when dealing with the most significant developments in the composition of time since 1900. By multidimensional and non-linear musical time I mean the superposition of several time layers, each moving at its own speed and more or less directionless. Beautiful examples are to be found in American art music from the beginning of the twentieth century onwards, especially in music by Charles Ives. The best known instances in Ives's music are, of course, *The Unanswered Question*, in which three layers of texture, pitch collections and time are superimposed, and the Symphony no. 4, in which sections in polytempo call for two conductors. In the case of Charles Ives, the superposition of time layers is usually motivated by programmatic ideas in general and childhood memories in particular. Past and present are combined simultaneously in a 'stream of consciousness', which makes Ives' music arguably the musical counterpart of Marcel Proust's *A la recherche du temps perdu* [17].

Music as directionless time, as epiphany, as an acoustic snapshot of a moment, or as fragment, is in marked contrast to the traditional goal-oriented, teleological concept of art music. It was in France that these ideas were developed further and that new concepts of musical time were explored in the context of philosophy and the philosophy of music. In a seminal essay, Gianmario Borio reconstructed the key

---

17. See Wolfgang Rathert, *Charles Ives* (Erträge der Forschung 267), Darmstadt 1989, pp. 22 and 62, which draws on earlier research by Frank R. Rossiter (*Charles Ives and His America*, New York 1975) and Martine Cardieu ('Charles Ives, or America of the "First Romance"', in: H. Wiley Hitchcock and Vivian Perlis (eds), *An Ives Celebration. Papers and Panels of the Charles Ives Centennial Festival Conference*, Urbana 1977, pp. 238-241).

factors in the unfolding of these new theories of musical time[18]. Pierre Souvtchinsky's distinction of psychological and ontological time was taken up by Gisèle Brelet, who elaborated the concept of 'objective', ontological time by relating it explicitly to compositional technique. By including elements of Henri Bergson's philosophy of time, Messiaen stressed the factor of perception: the 'durée vécue' — as counterpart of the 'temps structuré' — is not only present in the nineteenth-century Romantic music explicitly or implicitly criticized by Souvtchinsky and Brelet, but is also a factor in the perception of *all* music. In Table 1 below I have listed in binary opposition the concepts representative respectively of the new and the old views of musical time, as inspired by Borio's article and with my additions.

| *1. Philosophical categories* | |
|---|---|
| Ontological time | Psychological time |
| 'Temps espace' | 'Temps durée' |
| 'Temps structuré' | 'Durée vécue' |
| Dualistic | Monistic |
| Bergson | German idealistic philosophy (Hegel) |
| Being | Becoming |

| *2. Categories of time* | |
|---|---|
| Self-sufficiency | Development |
| Moment | Process |
| Non-linearity | Linearity |
| Discontinuity | Continuity |
| Reversibility | Irreversibility |
| Static | Dynamic |

| *3. Categories of musical composition and analysis* | |
|---|---|
| Proportion | 'Formenlehre' |
| Juxtaposition of sections | |
| Cutting/pasting/montage | |
| Constellation | |

*Table 1. Concepts of musical time in binary opposition*

---

18. Gianmario Borio, 'Kompositorische Zeitgestaltung und Erfahrung der Zeit durch Musik. Von Stravinskys rhythmischen Zellen bis zur seriellen Musik', in: Richard Klein, Eckehard Kiem and Wolfram Ette (eds), *Musik in der Zeit. Zeit in der Musik*, Weilerswirt 2000, pp. 313–332.

Strategies in composition and analysis subsumed under the heading of 'Formenlehre' in Table 1 are to be found in mainstream Central European art music of the nineteenth and (early) twentieth centuries. They include the way in which sections fulfil a specific formal function such as transition, secondary theme, coda etc. in the linear, one-dimensional temporal construction of a piece [19]. Although multidimensional sonata forms such as, for instance, Liszt's *B minor Sonata* (1852–1853) or Schoenberg's *First String Quartet* (1905) op. 7 or *First Chamber Symphony* (1906) op. 9 explore the limits of what is still possible in the 'Formenlehre' tradition, even these extreme examples embody the concept of process-driven, linear and goal-oriented music. A dualistic view of musical time acknowledges this concept but adds another one: non-linear, discontinuous music. Early examples in twentieth-century music of this alternative temporal frame of reference can be found in compositions by Claude Debussy and Stravinsky. Figure 2 comes from Jonathan Kramer's well-known analysis of Stravinsky's *Symphonies of Wind Instruments* (1920). Not only was this piece written to commemorate Debussy, the plural 'Symphonies' of its title points to the fact that Stravinsky distances himself from the tradition of the Austro-German symphony and its linear, teleological mould as well. As a consequence, Kramer does not name the individual sections of the work after functions in an overall formal process. He adopts the concept of 'moment', coined much later and in a different context by Karlheinz Stockhausen, to stress the fragmentation, self-sufficiency and non-linearity of the sections in these *Symphonies*.

In spite of what is suggested by the layout of Figure 2, the sections are not presented in a linear succession from A to G. On the contrary, they are interlocked in unpredictable ways. It should be underlined that a non-linear ordering calls for alternative constructional devices to create a coherent form. One way to achieve

---

19. The two most important publications in this field are the books by Erwin Ratz and William Caplin cited in footnote 5. In addition, James Hepokoski & Warren Darcy, *Elements of Sonata Theory: Norms, Types, and Deformations in the Late-Eighteenth-Century Sonata*, New York 2006, and Pieter Bergé (ed.), *Musical Form, Forms and Formenlehre. Three Methodological Reflections*, Leuven 2009, may be cited.

*Moment A*
Tempo I: ♪ = 144 (♩ = 72)

*Moment B*
Tempo II: ♩ = 108

*Moment C*
Tempo II: ♩ = 108

*Moment D*
Tempo II: ♩ = 108 (♩. = 72)

*Moment E*
Tempo I: ♩ = 72

*Moment F*
Tempo II: ♩ = 108 (♩. = 72)

*Moment G*
Tempo III: ♩ = 144 (♩. = 96)

*Figure 2. Overview of moments in Stravinsky's* Symphonies of Wind Instruments *(scheme from J. Kramer,* The Time of Music, *p. 255)*

this is to create proportional relationships between all tempi used, as in the *Symphonies*: 72:108:144, or 2:3:4.

As explained by Borio in the above-mentioned article, Messiaen's three laws of experienced duration ('trois lois sur la durée vécue') are instrumental in the importance attached to the perception of time by later composers of serial music. This is why they should be quoted here:

1. Experience of duration in the present: the more events in the present, the shorter our experience of duration for that moment in the present; the fewer events, the longer our experience of duration.

2. Retrospective evaluation of time passed: the more events in the past, the longer our experience of duration for that moment in the past; the fewer events in the past, the shorter our experience of duration for that moment in the past now.

3. The relation onset/duration: a short tone followed by a rest seems longer than a sustained tone of the same duration [20].

---

20. Olivier Messiaen, *Traité de rythme*, 1, p. 21: '1. Sentiment de la durée présente. Loi: Plus le temps est rempli, plus il nous paraît court — plus il est vide, plus il nous paraît long. 2. Appréciation rétrospective du temps passé. Loi inverse: Plus le temps était rempli, plus il nous paraît long maintenant — plus il était vide, plus il nous paraît court maintenant. 3. Loi des rapports attaques-durée: à durée égale, un son bref suivi d'un silence paraît plus long qu'un son prolongé'.

The first two laws—borrowed by Messiaen from the French philosopher Armand Cuvillier—apply to time in general, whereas the third law specifically deals with musical time. It is clear from this quotation that Messiaen, in contrast to Souvtchinsky, takes the psychological element of (musical) time seriously. His influence on the time concept and compositional techniques of Pierre Boulez, Jean Barraqué, Karel Goeyvaerts and Karlheinz Stockhausen can be observed in details of their rhythmic practice. Durations in the early serial works by these composers are measured by the IOI between attack points, regardless of whether the tone is sustained or split up into a tone ('positive value') and a rest ('negative value'). Furthermore, Messiaen's laws of perception of (musical) time have found their way into the theory of serial music. The title of the very first Stockhausen text on musical time ('Structure and Experienced Time'[21]) speaks for itself: the musical structure and more specifically the number and nature of musical events (see Messiaen) affect our perception of time. In these and other texts on his compositional craftsmanship Stockhausen belies the often-heard critique that serial music is focused on structural stringency, on intellectual calculation and constructivism only, without taking music perception into account. On the contrary, psychology and, in addition, physics are at the root of many new developments in the theory and practice of serial music during the 1950s. Gianmario Borio summarizes the importance of time perception for early serialism as follows:

> The theory of time that developed in the context of serial composition clarifies the enormous potential of the human psyche with regard to the experience of time. Opposing concepts such as periodic/aperiodic, successive/simultaneous, continuous/discontinuous, static/dynamic and goal-oriented/directionless are freed from their rigidity and are regarded as energetic forces within the composition itself[22].

---

21. Karlheinz Stockhausen, 'Struktur und Erlebniszeit' (1955), in: *Texte zur elektronischen und instrumentalen Musik* 1, Cologne 1963, pp. 86–98.
22. Borio, 'Kompositorische Zeitgestaltung', p. 329: 'Die Zeittheorie die im Umfeld des seriellen Komponierens entwickelt wurde, macht das enorme Potential des menschlichen Bewusstseins in Hinblick auf die Zeiterfahrung deutlich. Begriffsgegensätze wie periodisch/aperiodisch, sukzessiv/simultan, kontinuierlich/diskontinuierlich, statisch/dynamisch und zielgerichtet/richtungslos werden aus ihrer Starrheit gelöst und als Spannungsfelder der Komposition selbst betrachtet'.

In view of this, it comes as no surprise that Stockhausen would ultimately develop a theory of moment form in which an event in itself is considered as a temporal phenomenon, rather than a succession of events.

The fifth important development in the composition of time since 1900 is the elaboration of the TIME/SPACE CONTINUUM. The idea of a continuum suggests that pitch and duration are two dimensions of the same phenomenon: frequency (number of vibrations, number of beats per second) and that there is a continuity between these two dimensions. The best-known presentation of this theory is Stockhausen's famous text *...wie die Zeit vergeht...* (1956)[23]. Experiments with a pulse generator at the electronic music studio of the NWDR (Nord Westdeutsche Rundfunk) in Cologne led him to believe that a succession of isochronous pulses at a speed of 1/16 of a second or below results in rhythmic pulses and above that threshold, in pitch. Accelerating a sequence of equal durations turns rhythm into pitch, decelerating the frequency turns pitch into rhythmic pulse: 'micro-time' (pitch) and 'macro-time' (rhythm) are but two aspects of the same time/space continuum. Stockhausen's chromatic tempo scale was devised as a practical equivalent in the domain of duration to the chromatic pitch scale. However, the idea of this time/space continuum had been explored well before Stockhausen by Henry Cowell in one of the most visionary publications in the history of twentieth-century music theory[24]. The epistemological basis of Cowell's theory is hardly innovative, since he adopts the physical argumentation of the overtone series — the most widespread theoretical foundation of tonal harmony since Jean-Philippe Rameau — as the epistemological basis of his theory. But Cowell extends this received wisdom considerably, both in the domains of pitch

---

23. Published first in *die Reihe* 3, 1957, and later included in Karlheinz Stockhausen, *Texte* I, pp. 99–139.
24. Henry Cowell, *New Musical Resources*, New York 1930, was actually written in 1916–19. For an assessment of Cowell's original contribution to music theory, see Kyle Gann, 'Subversive Prophet: Henry Cowell as Theorist and Critic', in: David Nicholls (ed.), *The Whole World of Music. A Henry Cowell Symposium* (Contemporary Music Studies 16), Amsterdam 1997, pp. 171–222.

*Example 6. Overtone series on C; chorale; rhythmic structures derived from bb. 1, 2 and 9*[25].

---

25. From the Preface 'Composer's working notes on the *Quartet Romantic*' to the score of *Quartet Romantic* and *Quartet Euphometric* (Edition Peters No. 66518, 1974); also in: Dick Higgins (ed.), *Essential Cowell. Selected Writings on Music*, Kingston 2001, pp. 203–206.

and harmony and in the domains of rhythm and dynamics. To Cowell, tone clusters are as 'natural' as common chords since they are also extracted from the higher ranges of the series of partials. Cowell applies the overtone ratios to rhythm as well, as can be seen from Figure 3.

| Partial Series | Intervals | Tones | Relative Period of Vibration | | | | | Time |
|---|---|---|---|---|---|---|---|---|
| 5 | Third | E | \| 16 \| 16 \| 16 \| 16 \| 16 \| | | | | = 80 |
| 4 | Fourth | C | \| 16 \| 16 \| 16 \| 16 \| | | | | = 64 |
| 3 | Fifth | G | \| 16 \| 16 \| 16 \| | | | | = 48 |
| 2 | Octave | C | \| 16 \| 16 \| | | | | = 32 |
| 1 | Fundamental | C | \| 16 \| | | | | = 16 |

*Figure 3. The time/space continuum as exemplified by Henry Cowell (scheme from* New Musical Resources, *p. 47).*

The numbers under the heading 'Time' at the right of Figure 3 result from the multiplication of the number of vibrations per second of the fundamental tone $C$ (16) with the order number of the partial series at the left of this table. The C major chord created by the upper three pitches displays a periodicity of (3x16) + (4x16) + (5x16): the vibrations coincide at the beginning of the period, then separate to coincide once again at the end of the period. This is then transferred to the domain of rhythm, as can be seen from Figure 4.

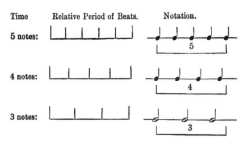

*Figure 4. Translation of the overtone frequencies to rhythm (scheme from* New Musical Resources, *p. 48).*

If the fundamental frequency equals a 4/4 beat, then the rhythms corresponding to the pitches from the C major chord are transcribed as the superposition of a minim triplet, four crotchets and a crotchet quintuplet, with the periodicities coinciding at the beginning of each bar.

In his *Quartet Romantic* (1917), written in the same period as *New Musical Resources*, Cowell derives the rhythmic structures from the ratios of the overtone series, as can be seen from Example 6. The time scale of the fifteen-bar chorale is multiplied by four in the *Quartet*: each crotchet note of the chorale yields an entire 4/4 bar in the *Quartet*. The bass tone *C* in the first bar of the chorale is the octave of the fundamental tone 1: overtone number 2 results in two minims. The chord of the first bar as a whole consists of the partial tones 2, 4, 5 and 6, translated by Cowell into the superposition of two minims, four crotchets, a quintuplet and a sextuplet of crotchets in the first four bars of the composition. The chords from the second bar of the chorale result in the superposition of $2^{2/3}$, 4, $5^{1/3}$ and $6^{2/3}$, followed by $2^{2/3}$, $4^{1/2}$, 6 and $7^{1/2}$, and the increase of the harmonic rhythm in bar 9 of the chorale is paralleled by the faster changing rhythmic periodicities in the last stave of the example. Note the use of fractions for the pitches/durations lacking in the overtone series (for example *F* situated between *C* (2) and *G* (3) and closer to the latter as $2^{2/3}$) and the use of triangular note heads devised by Cowell for the notation of components of triplets. Example 7 shows the opening bars of the *Quartet*, with its application of the rhythmic proportions from the first bar of the chorale and its free choice of pitches. The chords may be dissonant in this fragment, but the superposition of rhythms creates, according to Cowell, a 'perfect consonant', the rhythmic equivalent of a major triad.

Tempo relationships can be derived from the overtone series as well, as can be seen from Figure 5.

Pitches of the chromatic scale are expressed in ratios from *C* in the overtone series, and these ratios are applied to the 'fundamental' speed of 60 bpm, the result of which is a 'chromatic tempo scale'. Forty years later Stockhausen would come to comparable results.

*Example 7. Opening bars of H. Cowell's* Quartet Romantic *(1915–17)*
© *Edition Peters, New York.*

| Ratios from C | Tones of Chromatic Scale | | Equivalent M. M. Numbers |
|---|---|---|---|
| | C | = | 60 |
| 14 : 15 | C♯ | = | 64 2/7 |
| 8 : 9 | D | = | 67 1/2 |
| 5 : 6 | E♭ | = | 72 |
| 4 : 5 | E | = | 75 |
| 3 : 4 | F | = | 80 |
| 5 : 7 | G♭ | = | 84 |
| 2 : 3 | G | = | 90 |
| 5 : 8 | A♭ | = | 96 |
| 3 : 5 | A | = | 100 |
| 4 : 7 | B♭ | = | 105 |
| 8 : 15 | B | = | 112 1/2 |
| 1 : 2 | C | = | 120 |

*Figure 5. Overtone ratios applied to tempo*
*(scheme from* New Musical Resources, *p. 107).*

He starts from the same 'tempo octave' as Cowell (60 to 120), and the slight differences in the chromatic tempo steps can be explained by Cowell's use of partials in just intonation as the starting point of the calculations, whereas Stockhausen applies a logarithmic function ($^{12}\sqrt{2}$) in the context of equal temperament.

The last significant development in the composition of time that I want to discuss is the phenomenon of TIME FIELDS. By this I mean the situation in which an overall timespan is defined, but the order and duration of events taking place in this timespan is not. Early examples in which no exact synchronization of simultaneous events occurs are Stockhausen's woodwind quintet *Zeitmasse* (1955–56) and Witold Lutosławski's *Jeux vénitiens* (1961). In his woodwind quintet Stockhausen arranges different degrees of synchronization according to a series whose extremes are absolute synchronization — all five parts moving in the same speed; all five performers playing in the same tempo and metre — and total lack of synchronization — all five parts moving at different speeds; all five performers applying different tempi and different tempo modifications such as *accelerando* and *ritardando*; and the absence of a common beat or meter. As in other forms of serial organization, these extreme values are filled in with intermediary degrees of (a)synchronization. Lutosławski prefers to juxtapose blocks in which time is exactly coordinated between instruments playing in the same tempo and meter and blocks consisting of a collective temporal *ad libitum* in which pitch, dynamics and orchestration are prescribed but the synchronization between parts is not. Lutosławski developed an idiosyncratic notation for this so-called 'aleatoric counterpoint', a specimen of which can be seen in Example 8. The composer describes the notation procedures and the resulting time fields in the Preface to the score as follows:

> The *ad libitum* sections are not to be conducted. The beginning of each section is marked with an arrow which corresponds to the downbeat of the conductor. In the *ad libitum* sections all the rhythmic values are approximate. In consequence, the placing of the notes one above the other in the score does not necessarily mean that they are played simultaneously.

It is noteworthy that in this and other works, the composer keeps full control over the harmonic and formal organization of the work. Only the synchronization of the events within these time fields is entrusted to the laws of statistical (un)predictability. Other composers with a preference for large quantities of simultaneous and successive sound events, for instance, György Ligeti and Iannis Xenakis, also developed a penchant for time fields in which the listener perceives global movements of sound masses in time and space rather than discrete sound events. More generally,

# SYMPHONY No.3

Witold Lutosławski
(1983)

*Example 8. Opening of W. Lutosławski's Symphony no. 3 (1983)*
© *PWM Edition Kraków.*

the use of algorithmic procedures, in which a set of instructions is carried out in succession by a computer, is particularly suited for the composition of time fields. Stochastic algorithms generate large quantities of, in the case of fractals, self-similar sound events that are distributed in a non-ordered way over specific time fields.

These and similar developments made it clear that our rhythmic notation and performance practice had not kept up with the contemporary composer's imagination and thinking about musical time. Problems to do with the inadequacy of traditional music notation and of traditional performance practice are mutually related and have induced composers to use machines, making both performers and scores superfluous. It is no coincidence that the first electronic music studios came into being after the Second World War, at a time when composers were increasingly unhappy about the limitations of human performers and the inadequacy of the symbolic representation of the highly differentiated durations and sounds they had in mind. Conlon Nancarrow's player piano is another example of a machine that makes incredibly complicated temporal processes possible and audible not only for the inner ear of the composer but also for the listener. Nancarrow's *Studies for Player Piano* (1948-1992) are too diverse and rich to be summarized in a few words. Suffice it to say that as far as musical time is concerned, the use of this and similar machines has stretched the boundaries of the imaginable and the realizable to an unprecedented degree[26].

The inadequacy of traditional rhythmic notation has been only partially met by the introduction of alternative systems of nota-

---

26. I played Nancarrow's *Study for player piano no. 27* as an example during the Academy. In this piece gradual changes in tempo of the individual voices are specified in percentages (5%, 6%, 8% and 11%). One voice has a steady tempo ('the ticking of the ontological clock'), the other voices build a canonic texture in which the voices gradually speed up or slow down at the percentages mentioned. See Kyle Gann, *The music of Conlon Nancarrow* (Music in the Twentieth Century), Cambridge 1995, pp. 159-163. While it is true that Ligeti's *Etudes pour piano* have made possible the impossible in the domain of rhythm for many contemporary pianists, it is highly unlikely that a human performer will ever be able to play five different tempi simultaneously and to modify these tempi in the percentages indicated. On the other hand, since it is not my intention to glorify the use of machines for the presentation of music I hasten to add that other aspects of 'timing' (and also of articulation, sound production or rhetoric presentation) still require the sensitivity of a human performer.

tion. Time-space (or spatial, or proportional) notation, in which the horizontal distance between notes in the score is indicative of their duration, was used by, amongst others, John Cage. In his *Music of Changes*, Cage standardized the horizontal distance between notes with the same rhythmic value: two and a half centimetres of length equals one crotchet, and all other rhythmic values are derived from this equation by painstakingly measuring the horizontal distances between notes in the score. In doing so, Cage was able to notate the most complex a-metrical durations[27]. Problems of page layout, page turning and, not least, deciphering prevented time-space notation from becoming widely accepted, still less replacing traditional symbolic notation within contemporary music. Cage also introduced another type of notation entirely based on clock time, in which the metronome is substituted once and for all by the chronometer. Time brackets — defined by Cage as 'Time within which an action may be made'[28] — fix a timespan expressed in seconds and minutes. A sound event takes place within the timespan so defined. According to Rob Haskins, time-space and time brackets notations are inversionally related. Whereas in the former the relative placement of musical events in time is determined and the overall duration is not (necessarily), in the latter the duration is calculated to the second but the exact placement of the events in time is not[29]. In the beautiful series of so-called 'Number Pieces' written towards the end of his life John

---

27. See James Pritchett, *The music of John Cage* (Music in the Twentieth Century), Cambridge 1993, pp. 80–81.
28. This definition was formulated first in the performance instructions for Cage's *Theatre Piece* (1960) (see Paul van Emmerik, *Thema's en variaties: systematische tendensen in de compositietechnieken van John Cage*, Ph.D. dissertation, Department of Musicology, University of Amsterdam 1996, p. 61). This work 'consists of a fragmented series of actions distributed among random time frames' (Pritchett, *The music of John Cage*, p. 139). In contrast to the partially or entirely unspecified nature of the 'actions' in this and in following pieces (such as *0'00" (4'33" No. 2)*, 1962), the pieces with time brackets usually offer an exact definition of the pitch(es) to be played during the indicated time frame. This is the case in *Thirty Pieces for Five Orchestras* (1981), *Music for* (1984–1987) and for the series of Number Pieces beginning in 1987. I thank Jochem Valkenburg for his critical comments on the John Cage section of this chapter.
29. Rob Haskins, *'An anarchic society of sounds': The Number Pieces of John Cage*, Ph. D. dissertation, Department of Musicology, Eastman School of Music, University of Rochester 2004, p. 44.

Cage made use of flexible time brackets. Both the beginning and the end of a sound event are to be chosen freely by the performer within the timespans delineated by the flexible brackets (see Example 9).

# FOUR²

SOPRANOS                                                     John Cage

*Example 9. John Cage, Four ² (1990) for four-part choir; excerpt of the soprano part © Edition Peters, New York.*

Musical time in itself is amorphous. It takes a composer to mould time by compressing or stretching it, by using linear or non-linear strategies, by combining different layers of time simultaneously or not, by shaping time in a meaningful way. During the twentieth century composers developed new tools in the fields of rhythm, metre and tempo, tools that were successful in transcending the rather straightforward and schematic composition of time in previous music. However, the impact of our traditional notational system on musicians' imagination and performance of time should not be underestimated. With the exception of electronic music and music for machines, composers continue to use this traditional music notation. Reforms of musical notation remained idiosyncratic in spite of the fact that the centuries-old rhythmic notation has proved largely inadequate to represent the way musical time is often conceived and handled today. At the same time a lot of positive energy seems to result from staying within the system of notation transmitted from the past and from trying to work against its constraints. Perhaps composers struggling with this situation can take comfort from the conviction that a score is but a negative definition: it defines not what a musical work *is*, but — by exclusion — what it *is not*. When it comes to a non-idealistic, non-essentialist view of the musical work, the self-imposed or inherited restrictions in the notation of musical time beg for a creative interpretation by the performer(s) whilst at the same time respecting the composer's intentions.

# TEMPORAL COMPLEXITY IN MODERN AND POST-MODERN MUSIC: A CRITIQUE FROM COGNITIVE AESTHETICS

*Justin London*

---

*In Memoriam, Jonathan Kramer*

## 1.
## AESTHETIC RELEVANCE AND AUDIBILITY

Artworks, both musical and non-musical, have many properties—a sculpture may have a certain size and mass, which makes it a good paperweight; a piece of music may have a soothing effect which is therapeutically useful, and so on—but these properties are not usually thought of as aesthetically relevant. What are the aesthetically relevant properties of a musical artwork? An aesthetically relevant property is one which appertains to our experience, understanding, and critical appreciation of an artwork qua artwork—that is, music as music, and not music as sleep-aid.

To sort aesthetically relevant from aesthetically non-relevant properties of an artwork, one approach is to consider the notion of aesthetic function as recently critiqued and developed by Gary Iseminger (2004). Iseminger begins with a traditional view of the function of a work of art, as best expressed by Monroe Beardsley (1981). The gist of it is:

> The function of a work of art is to afford aesthetic experience.

As Iseminger points out, the problems with this approach are two (at least). First, nobody quite knows what a work of art is. Second, nobody quite knows what an aesthetic experience is (though we often have a good idea when we have one). To avoid these pitfalls, Iseminger approaches aesthetic experience from a slightly different tack:

The function of the practice of art is to promote aesthetic communication.
AND
A work of art is a good work of art to the extent it has the capacity to afford appreciation. (Iseminger 2004, p. 23)

Iseminger goes on to note that:

Appreciation is finding the experience of a state of affairs to be valuable in itself. (Iseminger 2004, p. 36)

To fully unpack all of these notions would require another article in its own right, but what I want to glean from them is that if we agree that artworks, as socially-entrenched states of affairs of a particular sort, afford appreciation, then this appreciation involves the *experience* of the artwork. Different genres of art are defined/ differentiated in large part in terms of the materials used in their composition, and correspondingly in terms of the sensory and cognitive faculties with which we perceive and understand them. We may thus relate aesthetic communication and aesthetic appreciation to these differentiae as follows:

Aesthetic experience and aesthetic communication are strongly tied to the experience of the primary medium of the work.

Without trying to define what exactly a musical work is, I think it reasonable to presume that musical works involve the organization and presentation of sounds in time—sound being the 'primary medium' of music. If the primary medium of music is that of sounds, then a proper experience of a musical work involves hearing those sounds. Thus, while musical scores may be interesting in their own right, their physical/visual properties are not of primary aesthetic relevance. Any relevance that the visual aspect of a score may have must supervene on the underlying experience of the music-as-heard. To put it another way, George Crumb's beautiful notation would not salvage a work that, when heard, we felt was musically defective. While we may have experiences of music that involve other senses (we may follow Crumb's score while we listen, we may watch an opera acted out on stage), it is always our aural experience of it that is key.

Moreover, this has to be a first person/first order aural experience of the music. While we may be interested in someone else's experience of a work (e.g., that of a good critic or analyst), we do not count such secondhand reports as a substitute for our own experience of a work. If the aesthetically relevant properties are tied to our first order experience of the medium of the work, then that experience is subject to our perceptual and cognitive limits as they pertain to that medium. And here is the problem for much modern, 'difficult,' 'complex,' or 'hyper-complex' music: many aspects of its structure and organization are not even remotely audible. With such music, extended score study is required in order for us to grasp even a fraction of what is going on. Indeed, the devotee of such music may spend far more hours to studying the score than actually listening to the piece. Even after such study, many aspects of the music's structure remain beyond our aural capacities. What, then, can their aesthetic relevance possibly be?

In the remainder of this article, I will explore the aesthetic relevance of rhythmic hyper-complexity. First, a portion of the psychological literature on auditory perception and cognition is reviewed in order to give the reader some idea of what kinds of rhythms we can and cannot hear. The role of metre in our experience of music, as a framework for rhythmic perception and understanding as well as a source of continuity, coherence, and motion, is also discussed. Next, the work of two composers, Olivier Messiaen and Milton Babbitt, is considered in relation to the limits on rhythmic perception just discussed. The emphasis here will be on precisely why and how certain structural premises and devices used by these composers lie beyond our perceptual capacities. The role of theoretical or analytical knowledge in our experience of music is then considered, drawing on the work of Mark DeBellis. This, in turn, leads to a consideration of the distinction between aesthetic and artistic properties, and the relationship between the two. The paper then concludes with rumination on the relationships between rhythmic complexity and artistic and aesthetic properties, and various sources of aesthetic value.

# 2.
# THE PERCEPTION OF RHYTHMIC DURATION,
# NUMBER, MOTION, AND COMPLEXITY

## 2.1 ORDER, DURATION AND NUMBER

There is a large body of work in auditory psychology dating back
to the nineteenth century that probes the limits and biases of
human hearing. For example, every musician knows that if a pair
of notes (say, the pianoforte middle C and the D above it) is
played in alternation, as the tempo increases one reaches a point
where the individual notes begin to blur. This, unsurprisingly, is
known as the 'trill threshold,' and for most listeners this blur
occurs at a tempo of around 10 notes per second. Likewise, if a
melody is played slower and slower, at some point it loses its sense
of coherence and motion, and becomes a series of isolated tones.
This happens for most listeners when the notes are more than
1.5–2.0 seconds apart[1].

Rhythm involves our perception of durations within a fairly narrow range—from 1/10 of a second (that is, 100 milliseconds or
'ms') to about two seconds. Within this range we are able to make
judgments regarding the number, order, and the relative, and
absolute duration of the elements in a rhythmic group. Consider,
for example, duration. In perceptual psychology the sensitivity of
any sensory modality is typically expressed in terms of the 'just
noticeable difference' or 'JND.' That is, given a stimulus of a certain magnitude (whether it is light intensity or color in vision,
duration or frequency in audition), how much change in a stimulus is necessary before such change becomes perceptually apparent?
As Dowling (1986) noted, in early studies of rhythm perception:

> The just noticeable difference between time intervals was measured in
> terms of subjects' precision in reproducing isolated intervals and in
> judging the relative durations of successive intervals in pairs ... But even

---

1. For more details on the 'speed limits' for musical rhythm, and their implications
for music theory and performance, see the author's *Hearing in Time*, (especially
Chapters 1 and 2).

at best, the JND size typically fell in the range of 5–10% (Woodrow 1951). This seemed enormous in comparison with JNDs for pitch, for example, which typically fall well under 1% … It has become apparent since 1950 that if the task is tapping along with a steady beat, listeners' precision is much better … with JNDs of the order of 2–3%" (p. 185).

Thus it is not only that we are able to make durational judgments within the 100ms to 2 second range; it is also that our rhythmic acuity is greatly enhanced in a metrical context (see also Drake & Botte 1993; Friberg and Sundberg 1995).

Our sensitivity to individual durations goes hand in hand with limits on our ability to categorize various durational patterns, both within and outside a metric context. Miller (1956) proposed the famous rule of 'seven plus or minus two' as a broadly applicable limit on our capacity for categorization. That we have a similarly limited number of durational categories was more recently shown by Desain and Honing (2003). In their study, they presented subjects with 66 variants on a 3-note figure, and then ask them to notate what they heard as precisely as possible. They found a strong tendency among subjects to employ only two basic rhythmic categories, a long and short, and so the four dominant figures were, as one might expect, Long–Short–Short, Short–Long–Short, Short–Short–Long, or as a series of nominally even durations. The 66 various stimuli were construed in terms of about a dozen basic patterns, all of which related to these four archetypes. Again, this categorization was enhanced when subjects were primed with a particular metric context.

It is important to note that within the range 1/10 to 2 seconds not all durations are alike. There seems to be a qualitative difference between durations less than about 1/3 of a second and those longer than about 1/3 of a second, what Paul Fraisse termed 'temps courts' and 'temps longs' (Fraisse 1956, Clarke 1999). Moreover, we have a preference for durations around 1/2 a second (James 1890, Parncutt 1994, van Noorden and Moelants 1999) — if there is a regular periodicity in or around this range, we are strongly drawn to it. Thus most musical rhythms, which mix short, medium, and long durations, involve qualitatively different 'kinds of time.'

In his essay 'Cognitive Constraints on Compositional Systems' Fred Lerdahl develops a number of desiderata—17 in all—for composing cognitively intelligible musical structures. These constraints are of two types, 'constraints on event sequences' and 'constraints on underlying materials.' The former focuses on hierarchical structure of the rhythmic surface and the creation of well-formed grouping structures, while the latter centres mostly on the nature of pitch materials. Lerdahl's event sequence constraints lay emphasis, perhaps too much emphasis, on regular accents and durational symmetry in the creation of well-formed rhythmic and metric structures. However, one can also look at 'constraints on underlying materials' in the temporal domain. For here is precisely where the limits on our perception and cognition of number and duration come into play. So, for example, constraint 10, 'intervals between elements of a collection arranged along a scale should fall within a certain range of magnitude' (p. 244) may be applied to durations, i.e., they all should be within the range of 1/10 to 2 seconds, as noted above.

### 2.2 MOTION

When presented with a series of undifferentiated clicks or tones, we nonetheless have a propensity to hear groups of twos or threes; this is known as *subjective rhythmicization* (Bolton 1894) or *subjective metricization* (London 2004). Likewise, when given a metrically ambiguous melody (one which, for example, could be heard either in duple or triple metre), we often experience a clear sense of a particular metrical organization on any given listening experience. We actively organize what we hear, based on innate perceptual and cognitive mechanisms, as well as on our habitual responses to familiar rhythmic stimuli. We do not hear a series of individual events, but patterns of *motion*, especially in the case of temporally continuous event sequences.

The philosopher Jerrold Levinson, drawing on the work of Edmund Gurney (1880), argues that musical experience is rooted in our grasp of these sorts of low-level patterns and their succession. He claims that 'To take satisfaction in some music is, above all, to enjoy following it, and its value as music ... [involves] an experience of following it over time that is intrinsically rewarding' (Levinson *Evaluating* 1996). Accordingly, Levinson's conception of *Basic Musical Understanding* essentially entails:

> [a] present-centered absorption in the musical flow; active following of musical progression; inward seconding of musical movement; sensitivity to musical alteration; continuational ability; and grasp of emotional expression (Levinson 1997, p. 32).

Note how much of Levinson's basic musical understanding is rhythmic in nature, as he speaks of our 'active following of musical progression.' Likewise we have and make use of an 'inward seconding of musical movement' as well as 'continuational ability' Levinson is describing both hearing music-as-motion and the phenomenon of *entrainment,* and I have argued that entrainment is the essence of musical metre:

> In many contexts we synchronize our attentional energies [and our motor behaviors] to the rhythms of the world around us. This synchronization is achieved by latching on to temporal invariants, that is, similar events that occur at regular intervals. Metre is a specifically musical instance of a more general perceptual facility of temporal attunement or entrainment. (London 2004, p. 25)

Thus not only is the presence of rhythmic regularity (and the metre it engenders) an aid to our durational discrimination, as noted above; it also is normative or prototypical for most styles and genres of music. To say that something is 'musical' implies, among other things, that it affords entrainment and hence gives rise to a sense of motion. Metre allows for musical understanding of a particular sort, as we may both (a) sense how it moves, and (b) move along with it. This is precisely the point made by Victor Zuckerkandl:

> Music contexts are *motion* contexts, kinetic contexts. Tones are elements of a musical context because and in so far as they are conveyors of a motion that goes through them and beyond them. When we hear music, what we hear is above all motions. (Zuckerkandl 1956, p. 76)

The motion we hear in music is of course illusory—it is, as Susanne Langer so aptly put it, the creation of 'virtual time' in a 'virtual space' (Langer 1953). But the fact that it may be illusory does not make it any less perceptually palpable. Indeed, as Robert Gjerdingen (1994) has noted, the perception of apparent motion in music (and other auditory phenomena) may involve the same neural mechanisms as motion perception in the visual domain.

To summarize, basic *rhythmic* understanding (pace Levinson) involves an awareness of the number of events present in a given amount of time (quantity) as well as their relative lengths (duration). We would not claim to 'understand' a rhythmic figure if we could not say whether it was a duplet or a triplet, or if it involved even or uneven durations. Likewise, our rhythmic engagement with music typically involves some degree of entrainment, which affords both the perception of motion as well as our ability to move with the music, either in our aural imagination or in fact. These are characteristic aspects of our experience of music.

## 2.3 RHYTHMIC COMPLEXITY

Both Jonathan Kramer (1988) and Fred Lerdahl (1988) have pointed out that musical complexity has to be structured in a certain way—hierarchically—in order for us to be able to comprehend it. Here is Kramer's example of how a hierarchical arrangement of pitches makes them readily graspable and memorable, while other orderings (which preserve the pitch-class content within each measure) do not:

*Figure 1.*

Here is a very simple rhythmic analogue, composed by the author:

*Figure 2.*

Figure 2a and Figure 2b use the same set of durations. In 2a there is a clear sense of duple metre stemming from the particular sequence of durations. Indeed, the patterning of durations allows the listener to infer an underlying pulse, as well as the implied 4/4 metre. The hierarchical organization of rhythm complements the metric context within which it is understood. Not so in Figure 2b. The juxtaposition of extremely short and extremely long durations at the outset forestalls any sense of intervening pulses, nor does any predictable grouping pattern ever emerge. Hierarchical structuring for rhythm thus is just as important as hierarchical structuring for pitch. With neither a palpable pulse nor a clear grouping structure, it is unlikely that any sense of metre or motion will emerge in 2b. In short, in most instances, intelligible rhythmic complexity involves the establishment of a metrical framework under which the configuration of durations can be understood.

# 3.
## MESSIAEN AND BABBITT: TWO CASE STUDIES IN RHYTHMIC COMPOSITION

Having argued that the aesthetically relevant properties of a musical artwork are tied to our first order experience of its primary medium — sounds in time — and having presented some empirical evidence as to the constraints of our rhythmic perception and cognition, the next step in my argument should be fairly obvious: the aesthetic success of a work cannot depend upon our experience of work's rhythmic structures if they involve distinctions or configurations which we cannot perceive. Here I will take up two cases, both more of compositional premises or systems rather than particular analyses, which seem to presume the unhearable: the duration series/scales used by Oliver Messiaen in his *Mode de valeurs et d'intensités*, and the use of a time-point series discussed by Milton Babbitt in his essay on 'Twelve Tone Rhythmic Structure' (and subsequently used by him and others). Others have noted the problems with these works (for a recent thorough critique and relevant bibliography see Taruskin 2005).

### 3.1 MESSIAEN'S *MODE DE VALEURS ET D'INTENSITÉS*

The score of *Mode de valeurs et d'intensités* tellingly includes tables of the articulative, dynamic, durational, and pitch palettes used in the construction of the piece. Here is my rendering of Messiaen's table of durational values used in *Mode de valeurs:*

Messiaen's 24 Durational Categories from *Mode de Valeurs*

Figure 3.

It is telling that Messiaen refers to these durations as 'chromatic degrees' (and thus as analogues to the order pitch classes of a chromatic scale). Messiaen used these materials in systematic combinations of rhythmic and melodic cells. Thus, in order to grasp these permutations and derivations, we have to be able to apprehend the presence of particular pitch, duration, attack, and intensity 'classes'—that a figure involves duration class 5 (quaver note tied to a demi-semiquaver) versus class 6 (dotted quaver)—as well as their more complex configurations.

Let us just consider Messiaen's duration series, apart from their interaction with pitch, attack, and intensity. From the outset it is clear that there are simply too many durational categories—well beyond the 'seven plus or minus two' limit noted above. Moreover, the 'chromatic degrees' of his various divisions require distinctions between categories well beyond our perceptual capacities.

Messiaen's tempo marking is 'Modéré — moderately. While not a metronome mark, if a crotchet is at 100 BPM, a reasonably central tempo marking for moderato, it would have a duration of 600ms. Thus a demi-semiquaver, the integer unit of Messiaen's duration scale, would have a duration of 75ms, and is probably too short to be heard as a rhythmic element. Likewise, the durational differences between categories are similarly slight (though, admittedly, above the JND threshold for most listeners). The fact that the piece does not often project a stable metre makes the JND threshold for durations even higher.

Messiaen himself seemed aware of the impossibility of hearing such fine-grained aspects of *Mode de valeurs*, as he noted that these sorts of structures convey a 'charm of the impossibilities,' (*Technique,* p. 21), of musical 'facts' to be known with our minds, if not our ears. Taruskin's comment on this piece is most apt in this regard:

> The music consists of a ceaseless 'counterpointing' of elements drawn from the stringently limited menu [of pitches and durations] just described, individual hypostasized objects in seemingly fortuitous relationships ... One may fairly wonder why Messiaen would have wished to court an impression of randomness; or (perhaps more to the point) why one would wish to plan such an apparently haphazard outcome in such meticulous detail ... In the case of Messiaen himself, answers are probably to be sought in his religious philosophy, in which the incomprehensible results of unknowable plans can symbolize the relationship of man and God. (Taruskin 2005, vol 5, pp. 25–26)

### 3.2 BABBITT ON 'TWELVE TONE RHYTHMIC TECHNIQUE'

In his 1962 essay on 'Twelve Tone Rhythmic Structure' Milton Babbitt was critical of interpreting durations as analogues to scale steps, as he notes that 'the temporal analog of pitch interval is translatable only as the 'difference between durations'' (Babbitt 1962/1972, p. 161). Instead, he draws an analogy between pitch organization and metre, and gives the following example:

Metric time-point series, after Babbitt (1972) ex. 6.1:

*Figure 4.*

In each measure of 6/8 in Figure 4 one may identify twelve attack points (at the level of the semiquaver), and these attack points may be regarded as analogues to an ordered collection of chromatic pitch classes. As such, this example displays the following time point (or 'attack point') series: [0,3,11,4,1,2,8,10,5,9,7,6], putatively isomorphic to a tone row of analogous pitch classes. There are several problems, however, in approaching the rhythmic structure of this passage in this way. First, as this pattern of attack points does not clearly indicate the presence of 6/8 to the listener, there is little, if any, way for him or her to grasp the time-point series, as he or she would lack the appropriate metric index. Even if 6/8 were readily apparent (imagine this with a click track or other percussive underpinning), we don't perceive a filling of the metric aggregate in a manner analogous to filling the pitch class aggregate. This is because in a metric context, the intervening attack points over the course of a long duration are still present as part of the listener's *entrainment* in a way that intervals between widely separated pitches are not. Babbitt is aware of these difficulties, as he notes that there are 'manifest differences between the elements of the pitch system and those of the time-point system, that is, perceptual — not formal — differences' (p. 162, and see also his remarks on repetition, p. 163–164). But a larger problem looms. For metre itself is hierarchical, and so we grasp these time points in a hierarchically-structured way. Thus rather than a sense of an attack 'at time point 7' (in this example, this attack occurs in the 5th measure), we rather hear such an articulation as occurring on 'the second subdivision of the first 8th that itself is a subdivision of beat two.' Babbitt's non-hierarchical index of time point locations does not match with the way we hear temporal locations in a metrical context[2].

### 3.3 OTHER ASPECTS OF RHYTHMIC COMPOSITION
### AND DEVELOPMENT

We are on somewhat firmer ground if we think of a more familiar melody or rhythm, and then speak of it undergoing some sort of global transformation, such as retrograde, transposition (moving a rhythmic figure about in a measure), augmentation or diminution. These are familiar compositional devices. However, they too have their limitations, as John Sloboda (1985) has shown:

*Figure 5.*

Sloboda used these two versions of the 'same' melody in an experiment which studied how notation led the performers to use different patterns of expressive timing to make the metric orientation of each version of this tune clear. From a set-theoretic point of view, Figure 5b is a simple 'transposition' of 5a by one unit of subdivision. But in the course of Sloboda's experiment, where these two versions were presented interleaved with other melodies, *none* of his subjects noticed that 5b was a 'transposition' of 5a. On a more basic level, one cannot transpose, retrograde, or rotate elements time-series in the same way as a pitch series. A permutation of a Long–Short–Short rhythm results in a syncopation, and as Gjerdingen (1993) has noted, retrogrades of rhythms, especially as they are actually performed, often induce radically different perceptions.

Thus it would seem that Messiaen's and Babbitt's careful and systematic rhythmic designs are in large part, for naught, for in the

---

2. The hierarchical indexing of time points in a measure noted here might be related to the hierarchical organization of pitch alphabets proposed by Lerdahl (see his *Tonal Pitch Space*, especially his 'basic space' for pitch-classes, pp. 47w59).

case of the former, there are too many categories (and they are too finely drawn), while in the case of the latter, we do not relate metre to pitch in the manner suggested. Therefore these details and isomorphisms cannot be part of our first-order experience of the primary medium of these compositions. Can they still have any aesthetic relevance?

# 4.
## ANALYTICALLY-INFORMED LISTENING (?)

An obvious rejoinder to the argument developed this far is that we do not and need not know music by our ears alone. We read essays by the composers, analyses by music theorists, and study scores ourselves. Surely our knowledge of structural relationships, gained from our second order experience of the work (analyses, commentary, score study) will enable us to appreciate at least some of these relationships and structures, and thus affect our first order experience of the work. Mark DeBellis (1995) has considered these issues in some detail. In his discussion, DeBellis draws on a previous essay by Peter Kivy which invokes the characters of Tibby and Mrs. Munt from E.M. Forster's novel *Howard's End* listening to Beethoven's *Fifth Symphony* (Kivy 1990). Tibby is the listener who is 'profoundly versed in counterpoint, and holds the score open on his knee,' while Mrs. Munt can only 'tap surreptitiously when the tunes come.' Tibby listens with a full knowledge of structure and theory; Mrs. Munt has nought but her innocent ears.

DeBellis characterizes certain aspects of Tibby's versus Mrs. Munt's experience of the music in this way:

> Tibby knows that closure is explained by reference to scale-step properties. Hence, not only does he hear the music coming to a close, and hear the arrival of the tonic, but he hears the closing with an appreciation of the way it depends on the tonic's arrival. For this reason, his [listening experience] has a coherence not present in the experience of someone who is unaware [of those properties, such as Mrs. Munt] (p. 126).

Tibby is DeBellis's exemplar of a *theoretically-informed listener*. By listening under the framework of music-theoretical knowledge, Tibby 'has a deepened perception of a structural property for what it is, and that is central to his increased appreciation [of it]' (p. 129). In the case of Messiaen and (perhaps especially) Babbitt, analytical knowledge of the piece may allow the listener at least to grasp more of the relevant structural features, if only by making a greater effort to hear them. Even if one cannot aurally grasp particular features (e.g., durational categories, time point series), one still has a sense of what is behind the surface effects that one can hear.

However, DeBellis goes on to note that while this account has some plausibility, two important objections can be made to it. First, it is not clear why we ought to count the understanding Tibby derives from know the explanatory connection as an understanding *of the music* rather than of how the music *is* or *works*. While sensitivity to consonance and dissonance, or durational distinctions is surely essential to musical understanding, it is doubtful that knowledge of their physical basis in frequency ratios, specific durational proportions, or time-point indices is essential. Second, if our aesthetic posture towards a work consists in appreciating the way feature *A* depends on feature *B*, then it had better be the case that one really does depend on the other. To put it another way, theoretically informed musical pleasure is subject to a certain defeasibility. Were we to learn that a certain rhythmic repetition does not explain coherence — for example, if a slightly different pattern (one which does not have the dependency relationship noted above) sounds just as coherent — then a pleasure taken in that supposed connection would be shown to be in a certain sense unjustified. (DeBellis, pp. 130–131).

This 'defeasibility' is precisely where empirical studies of musical perception and performance gain purchase. For if slight alterations (in durational ratios, for examples) were to go unnoticed, or if they cannot even be performed in the first place, then analytical or theoretical accounts of the compositional complexity of a piece based on such relationships cannot account for a piece's aesthetic value (or lack thereof). One cannot have a 'deepened perception for what something is' if one cannot have even a shallow perception in the first place.

DeBellis' original case of theory-laden hearing presumes that there are perceptible structures upon which a theory may or may not gain a purchase. And, indeed, his main point seems to be that what music theories and analyses typically do is give the listener a greater and more nuanced awareness of what is there to be heard. That is, given the perception of two different pitches, or rhythms, or other structural configurations, a theory will tell us how they are different and in what ways they are alike, and may (perhaps) lead us to hear a structural relation where we did not. What theories do not aim to do is to make perceptually indiscernible identicals discernible.

At this point, we have arrived at a place where the appreciation of such musical works depends not on our experience of them, but on our second-order knowledge of their structure, their means of production, and the composer's aesthetic aims. This is not so much an appreciation of the musical works, but of the composer's intentions and motivations behind such works. As such, the music of high Modernism becomes conceptual art: works (that is, scores) are to be seen but not necessarily heard. Performances of such works serve as demonstrations or authentications that simply allow one to say that such-and-such a piece of music has an existence as sounding music.

## 5.
## AESTHETIC VERSUS ARTISTIC PROPERTIES

Having backed DeBellis into a corner, another distinction is in order. That is the distinction between *aesthetic* and *artistic* properties of an artwork. This distinction originates with Frank Sibley (1959, 1965); here is a more recent definition from Davies:

> *Aesthetic properties* are usually characterized as objective features perceived in the object of appreciation when it is approached for its own sake. Such properties are internal to the object of appreciation. They are directly available for perception in that their recognition does not require knowledge of matters external to the object of appreciation. In particular, their recognition does not depend on information about the

circumstances under which the item was made or about its intended or possible [non artistic] functions. (Davies 2006, 53–54)

Aesthetic properties are characterized by adjectives like 'unified,' 'balanced,' 'dynamic,' 'powerful,' 'graceful,' 'delicate,' 'elegant,' or 'beautiful' (Davies 2006, p. 54)[3]. By contrast, *artistic properties* require the mediation of knowledge about the artist or artwork under appreciation; as such they are characterized by adjectives like 'innovative' (or its negative, 'derivative'), 'transgressive,' 'symbolic,' 'metaphoric,' and so on. Artistic properties often involve the relation of a work to traditions of style, genre, and medium. For example, there are conventions of representation (e.g., a painting that involves woman with a dove hovering on her shoulder is a representation of the Annunciation), of quotation or allusion (e.g., the use of the 'Dies Irae' in Berlioz's *Symphonie Fantastique*), and so forth. Many, if not most, artworks involve both aesthetic and artistic properties, and (at least according to some philosophies of art), a full experience and understanding of a work of art involves both. That is to say, without knowledge of iconography you may see a man and a funny lizard, but not grasp that it is St. George and the Dragon, nor will you understand that number of measures in the 'Crucifixus' from Bach's *B-minor Mass* is a representation of the number of steps Christ traversed on the Via Dolorosa.

Theories and analyses of musical structure of the sort DeBellis details tend to deal with 'properties directly available for perception' whose 'recognition does not require knowledge of matters external to the object of appreciation.' As such they are more concerned with aesthetic than artistic properties of works. Indeed, music theorists and analysts have largely left considerations of artistic properties to historical musicologists and music critics. Of course there are exceptions — George Perle's analysis of Berg's *Lyric Suite* immediately comes to mind — but even in this case,

---

3. Note that works may embody different aesthetic properties of differing degrees of relevance. The audible properties of George Crumb's music and the visual properties of his scores may both be regarded aesthetic properties although, as noted above, the former usually take precedent over the latter in terms of relevance.

while there may be hidden meanings and symbolism, it is usually claimed that the primary value of such works comes from their aesthetic properties. Moreover, it is usually presumed that our grasp of artistic properties comes from our first-order experience of the work in combination with our knowledge of its historical and artistic context. For example, when we hear the 'Dies Irae' in Berlioz's *Symphonie Fantastique,* it is our ears that tell us the borrowed tune is there. Our prior knowledge allows us to identify the tune, and know its religious significance. But we are not dependent on second order knowledge for our grasp of these artistic properties.

## 6.
## ARTISTIC ASPECTS OF RHYTHMIC COMPLEXITY

Works can fail artistically, but succeed aesthetically, and vice-versa. For example, one may paint an aesthetically successful watercolour of a woman and child (well balanced, vibrant colors, animate faces, etc.), which fails as a representation of the Madonna and Child because it botches the necessary symbolic conventions. Conversely, one may succeed in one's artistic intentions (e.g., I will write a piece that contains allusions to and quotations from Wagner's *Ring Cycle*) and nonetheless produce a work which fails aesthetically (the piece is a horrible motley). Notice, however, that there is an implicit asymmetry here. While an aesthetic success usually makes for a good work of art, whether or not the artistic aims are fulfilled (our failed representation of the Madonna may nonetheless be a good figure painting, for example), the converse is not true. A successful representation of the Madonna, iconographically correct, may nonetheless have so many flaws in perspective, composition, rendering of the figure, and so forth, as to make the painting a failure (and indeed, something one can identify as a 'very bad attempt at painting the Madonna').

It may help to recall Iseminger's remarks about artworks and our experience of them given at the start of this essay: 'A work of art is a good work of art to the extent it has the capacity to afford appreciation;' 'Aesthetic communication occurs when someone makes a work with the aim that someone else appreciate it;' and 'Appreciating is finding the experience of the work to be valuable in itself.' On this view, appreciation is grounded in the experience of the work, and by 'capacity to afford appreciation' I take Iseminger to mean (or at least strongly to imply) that this 'capacity' is grounded in an artwork's ability to afford a valuable first-order experience of it. In short, it is grounded on aesthetic properties. Were this not the case, then the asymmetry between positive aesthetic and artistic properties noted above would not hold: so long as a work afforded appreciation under *any* mode of experience of it, we would have to grant that it has value as an artwork.

Here, then, is a compositional thought-experiment. Consider my *Subtle Etude #1*, a piece consisting wholly of a series of long, repeated tones (the particular pitch is not important). The tones should sound identical, but really are not, as they involve minute differences in duration and dynamics. The score might begin like this:

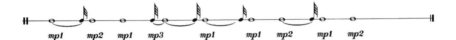

*Figure 6.*

The score uses only three classes of durations (in a quasi-random order), and at the given tempo (crotchet = 40 beats/minute), each note is six seconds long (or slightly more; the hemidemisemiquaver adds about 23 milliseconds of duration, for example). Likewise there are three dynamic levels, and here I will stipulate that each differs by .2 decibels. These distinctions have been chosen because they fall well below our ability to perceive them (the JND for volume is approximately 1 db, and for unmetred duration roughly 5% of the inter-onset interval—here about 300 ms—though durational discrimination is very poor for intervals greater than about 2 seconds).

Now consider two performances of this piece. One performance is a MIDI realization, with precise control of the durations and dynamics indicated in the score. In a computer realization, what you see is what you hear, even though you can't hear it. Any distinctions we think we might hear in listening to the MIDI realization will be misperceptions, perhaps influenced by the presence of the score. The other performance would involve a human performer. The human performer faithfully tries to realize the score, with the paradoxical constraint that if she should make any note audibly longer or louder, it would be a mistake. In the latter context, any durational or dynamic differences we might hear could be either (a) figments of our musical imaginations, as in the MIDI performance, or (b) performance mistakes. But we may not be able to tell which is which. Furthermore, it is likely that there will be mistakes, as this is an impossible performance task. But that impossibility is precisely the point.

What sort of appreciation is afforded by our experience of this piece? If we were to hear the MIDI version piece without knowing its premise, I presume we would find it extremely boring. We are likely to find the 'live' version of the piece also quite boring on a naïve listening. If we do know the premise of the piece, we may find a performance interesting—at least part of a performance, perhaps at least once. I doubt, however, if most listeners would care to hear the piece a second time. While the piece might be said to raise a number of interesting artistic questions—about the nature of 'subtlety' in structure or performance; about effable and ineffable aspects of performance; about the limits of human control in performance, and so forth—engaging these questions does not require much in the way of first-order experience of the piece. Its subtlety foregrounds the perceptual problems involved in grasping its admittedly modest structure. But that, again, is more an appreciation of the premise behind the piece than of the piece itself.

If this subtle étude is too subtle and too simple to be heard, it is an analogue to hyper-complex works—and of course, I have posited it for that very reason. By their very nature, hyper-complex works will tend to maximize artistic properties—what we might regard as aspects of compositional design or method—at the expense of aesthetic properties. That is, whatever aesthetic properties such works have in a particular musical parameter (rhythm, pitch, timbre), they have as a result of the 'gross morphology' of that parameter that results indirectly from the more minute underlying structure. Our perceptual and cognitive limitations block our direct access of such complex structural details, and hence we are unable to infer these complex artistic properties from our first order experience of the work. However, this does not forestall a positive experience of those *aesthetic* properties of such works that are experientially accessible: what we can hear may well be rhythmically engaging, display formal balance, have varied musical colours, and so forth.

In hyper-complex music we often hear an effect without a clear grasp of its cause. We all become like Mrs. Munt in our experience of the work—our prior musical expertise as performers or composers (or even music theorists) is of little avail. Indeed, this seems just what Messiaen means when he speaks of the 'strange charm of impossibilities' noted above:

> In spite of himself he [the listener] will submit to the strange charm of impossibilities: a certain effect of tonal ubiquity in the nontransposition, a certain unity of movement (where beginning and end are confused because identical) in the non-retrogradation, all things which lead him progressively to that sort of *theological rainbow* which the musical language, of which we seek edification and theory, attempts to be. (*Technique*, p. 21; quoted in Taruskin, vol. 4, p. 235)

In this quotation from his *Technique of my Musical Language*, Messiaen is specifically referring to his modes of limited transposition for pitch and his palindromic (non-retrogradable) rhythms, but the 'confusion' here is of a piece with the effect of the pitch and durational organization of *Mode de valeurs*. Messiaen's aim here is not the production of complexity with a view to our grasping it. His point is a religious one. Here is Taruskin's apt summary of Messiaen's theological aims:

> Many of the rhythmic techniques Messiaen describes ... [involve] durational plans that could be mentally conceptualized but not followed perceptually ... Like the truths of astronomy and many other scientific truths (as well, needless to say, as religious truths), it is the sort of fact

that reflective intellect reveals sooner than the senses. Putting such a thing into an artwork is an implicit warning against assuming that true knowledge can only be gained empirically. The highest truths, Messiaen's music implies, are revealed truths. Theology was truth. Anything beyond that, Messiaen implied ... was mere history.' (vol. 4, p. 236)

Messiaen's complexity is a means of pointing musically to transcendence. We are meant to be overwhelmed by the complexity of his music, not to grasp it. Our resultant listening experience will be fragmentary and/or incoherent. Richard Shusterman has noted that such experiences may also have a kind of aesthetic value:

> We appreciate such art because it disturbs our sense of order and gives us a feeling of shock and disruption that we find somehow valuable (interesting, challenging, therapeutic, refreshing, and so forth) ... Such experience, though not coherent or complete, displays at least the integrity of standing out as a distinctly singular experience, in contrast to the stream of ordinary experience' (Shusterman 2006 p. 222).

This may be true and, if anything, such musical experiences are a reminder of the 'phenomenal fragility' of music: as an art of sound in time, we presume it must involve sounds we can hear, whose shape we can grasp, and whose organization we can remember. But sometimes we cannot hear, we cannot grasp, we cannot remember. Hyper-complex musical forms are not just challenges to the listener (or performer), but to the very notion of what properly constitutes the musical artwork itself.

## WORKS CITED

– Babbitt, Milton, 'Twelve Tone Rhythmic Structure and the Electronic Medium', in: Benjamin Boretz & Edward T. Cone (eds.), *Perspectives on Contemporary Music Theory*, New York 1971, pp. 148–79.
– Beardsley, Monroe, *Aesthetics, Problems in the Philosophy of Criticism*, 2nd edition, Indianapolis, 1981.
– Bolton, Thomas L., 'Rhythm', in *American Journal of Psychology* 6 (1894), pp. 145–238.
– Clarke, Eric. 'Rhythm and Timing in Music', in: Diana Deutsch (ed.), *The Psychology of Music*, 2nd Edition, New York 1999, pp. 473–500.
– Davies, Stephen, *The Philosophy of Art*, Oxford 2006.
– DeBellis, Mark, *Music and Conceptualization*, Cambridge 1995.
– Desain, Peter, and Henkjan Honing, 'The Formation of Rhythmic Categories and Metric Priming', in: *Perception* 32 (2003) 3, pp. 341–65.
– Dowling, W. Jay, and Dane L. Harwood, *Music Cognition*, Orlando 1986.
– Drake, Carolyn, and Marie-Claire Botte, 'Tempo Sensitivity in Auditory Sequences: Evidence for a Multiple-Look Model', in: *Perception and Psychophysics* 54 (1993) 3, pp. 277–86.
– Fraisse, Paul, *Psychology of Time*, New York 1963.
– Friberg, Anders, and Johan Sundberg, 'Time Discrimination in a Monotonic, Isochronous Sequence', in: *Journal of the Acoustical Society of America* 98 (1995) 5, pp. 2524–31.
– Gjerdingen, Robert O., 'Apparent Motion in Music?', in: *Music Perception* 11 (1994) 4, pp. 335–70.
– ———, '"Smooth" Rhythms as Probes of Entrainment', in: *Music Perception* 10 (1993) 4, pp. 503–08.
– Gurney, Edmund, *The Power of Sound*. London 1880.
– Iseminger, Gary, *The Aesthetic Function of Art*, Ithaca NY 2004.
– James, William, *The Principles of Psychology* (Dover Reprint), New York 1890/1950.
– Kivy, Peter, *Music Alone*, Ithaca NY 1990.
– Kramer, Jonathan D., *The Time of Music*, New York 1988.
– Langer, Susanne, *Feeling and Form*, New York 1953.
– Lerdahl, Fred, 'Tonal Pitch Space', in: *Music Perception* 5 (1988) 3, pp. 315–50.
– ———, *Tonal Pitch Space*, New York 2001.
– ———'Cognitive Constraints on Compositional Systems' in the *Contemporary Music Review*, 1992, vol. 6. (Harwood Academic Publishers GmbH)
– Levinson, Jerrold, 'Evaluating Music', in: *Revue Internationale de Philosophie* 198 (1996), pp. 593–614.
– ———, *Music in the Moment*, Ithaca NY 1997.
– London, Justin, *Hearing in Time*, New York 2004.
– Messiaen, Oliver, *Etudes de rythme. Mode de valeurs et d'intensités*, Paris 1950.
– Miller, George A., 'The Magic Number Seven, Plus or Minus Two: Some Limits on Our Capacity for Processing Information', in: *Psychological Review* 63 (1956), pp. 81–97.
– Parncutt, Richard, 'A Perceptual Model of Pulse Salience and Metrical Accent in Musical Rhythms', in: *Music Perception* 11 (1994) 4, pp. 409–64.
– Schaeffer, Pierre, *Traité des objets musicaux: essai interdisciplines*, Paris 1977/1966.
– Scruton, Roger, *The Aesthetics of Music*, Oxford 1997.

– Shusterman, Richard, 'Aesthetic Experience: From Analysis to Eros', in: *Journal of Aesthetics and Art Criticism* 64 (2006) 2, pp. 217–29.
– Sibley, Frank, 'Aesthetic Concepts', in: *Philosophical Review* 68 (1959), pp. 421–450.
– ————, 'Aesthetic and Non-Aesthetic', in: *Philosophical Review* 74 (1965), pp. 135–59.
– Sloboda, John A., 'The Communication of Musical Metre in Piano Performance', in: *Quarterly Journal of Experimental Psychology* 35A (1983), pp. 377–96.
– van Noorden, Leon, and Dirk Moelants, 'Resonance in the Perception of Musical Pulse', in: *Journal of New Music Research* 28 (1999) 1, pp. 43–66.
– Woodrow, Herbert, 'The Effect of Rate of Sequence Upon the Accuracy of Synchronization', in: *Journal of Experimental Psychology* 15 (1932) 4, pp. 357–79.
– Zuckerkandl, Victor, *Sound and Symbol: Music and the External World*, New York 1956.

# RHYTHMS – DURATIONS – RHYTHMIC CELLS – GROUPS. CONCEPTS OF MICROLEVEL TIME-ORGANISATION IN SERIAL MUSIC AND THEIR CONSEQUENCES ON SHAPING TIME ON HIGHER STRUCTURAL LEVELS

*Pascal Decroupet*

In his 1944 publication *Technique de mon langage musical,* Olivier Messiaen initially studied rhythm, then pitch. This seems to be an inversion of the usual approach in Western music theory since most theories until then were primarily based on considerations related to pitch-organization, be it melody, phrase-structure or harmony. For Messiaen, rhythm reached a degree of independence that allowed the consideration of this dimension on its own, even if in the first chapter, 'Charme des impossibilités et rapport des différentes matières', it is precisely the relationship between the dimensions of pitch and rhythm on which Messiaen focussed. Taking as examples two particularly interesting 'impossibilities', modes of limited transposition and non-retrogradable rhythms, he immediately stressed their analogies: 'les rythmes réalisent dans le sens horizontal (rétrogradation) ce que les modes réalisent dans le sens vertical (transposition)' (vol. 1, p. 5 — 'the rhythms realizing in the horizontal direction (retrogradation) what the modes realize in the vertical direction (transposition)', English translation, vol. 1, p. 13).

As shown by his first examples (taken from Igor Stravinsky's *The Rite of Spring* or the treatise on Hindu rhythms by Çârngadeva written in the thirteenth century), Messiaen is interested in *rhythms,* that is to say, in groups of durations with characteristic properties. (To avoid the usual vocabulary of motives and themes in the domain of rhythm, he sometimes uses the term *personnages rythmiques.*) These rhythms may undergo specific transformations such as more or less regular augmentations and diminutions (vol. 1, p. 10–11; vol. 2, p. 3–4), but also inner permutations (i.e. an exchange of the place of specific values in the rhythm) or subdivisions of specific durations (what Messiaen calls *monnayage*). All these techniques are very prominent in the *Quatuor pour la Fin du Temps*: the text given there as a preface anticipates certain pages of his *Technique*.

In the 1948 solo-piano piece *Cantéyodjayâ* (first performed in 1954), Messiaen took a decisive step for mid-twentieth century music history, since at its sixth tempo-indication (p. 8 of the score, bars 64–101), *Modéré*, he presented a 'mode de durées, de hauteurs et d'intensités', combining three layers of eight pitches each with a different duration and a specific dynamic level.

*Example 1.*

The harmonic structure of the first layer of this mode (all eight notes are given once each to begin with) only differs from the fourth mode of limited transpositions by a single note (B-flat instead of G), and while the *pp*-figure combining the first four notes evolves linearly in register by a continuous descending movement, the *ff*-figure grouping the four last notes alternates with downwards and upwards directed movements (the connection between both figures initially breaks the regularity of the descending movement). The second layer conforms completely with the fourthmode, but while the last two pairs express the structural tritone-relation explicitly (A-flat rising to D, A falling to E-flat), the two pairs are interlaced in the first segment of four notes (F/E/B/B-flat). The first D of this second layer has to be considered as an anticipation, its role is to emphasize (one octave lower than the initial D of the first layer) the structural tritone-

70

relation of the first segment of layer I as well as to connect both layers precisely through another tritone-relation. Here, the two occurences of the D on the one hand function as two members of the same pitch-class (the second revealing a harmonic relationship the first one does not express through melodic adjacency until bar 70 — see also bars 72 and 74), on the other hand these occurences manifest them as two different 'sound-objects' (since there is no other characteristic in common with them: *pp* becomes *p*, and the duration changes from a demisemiquaver to a dotted crotchet). The third layer, harmonically, also contains strong tritone-relations since it displays a second mode (i.e. an octatonic scale) with only one alteration (A-flat instead of A). The last note of this layer, the G-sharp, occurs only in bar 78, after a first repetition of the only clearly expressed tritone-relation (in succession as in register-repartition) of this layer; this tritone B-flat/E is often combined with the C-sharp in the same register, thus expressing prominently one of the ic3-cycles founding the octatonic scale.

The durations Messiaen considered them really as isolated values since he no longer used the word rhythm — evolve regularly by addition of the shortest value in the upper layers: in layer I, from a demisemiquaver to a crotchet, in layer II from a semiquaver to a minim (beginning with the second note, the F — see above). Layer III combines pairs of durations evolving 'from the extremes to the centre' with one supplementary permutation between the values 5 and 6. While layer I displays a regular repartition of the two used dynamic levels (*pp* and *ff*), layer II functions by pairs involving three complementary dynamics (*p-mf-f*); layer III refers only to the two extreme dynamics (*pp* and *ff*), but irregularly, the grouping densities restricting progressively (4-2-1-1), an eventual analogy to the 'from the extremes to the centre'-strategy in the domain of durations.

This passage clearly anticipated the piece that has gained celebrity in music history as one of the essential precursors of integral serialism, that is the *Mode de valeurs et d'intensités*, composed in Darmstadt in 1949, where Réné Leibowitz was present for the second time to lecture on Arnold Schoenberg's Viennese School (his book *Schoenberg et son école* had been published in French in 1947 and translated into English as early as 1949). The preface to the *Mode* is probably far better known than the composition itself, as Messiaen explained there the work's modal strategy by separating the acoustic dimensions: twelve values for articulation (attack); seven values for dynamics; three divisions of twelve chromatic durations each, beginning respectively with a demisemiquaver, a semiquaver and aquaver; and, finally, three pitch divisions each exploring the chromatic pc-reservoir. Two remarks need to be made here. 1) The reason why Messiaen combined the durations into a complete sequence of twenty four values has never been convincing to me, since *hierarchally* the crotchet as the eighth value of division I, the fourth value of division II and the second value of division III, *is not* the same duration, especially as all dimensions are connected in a stable way throughout the composition. 2) All three pitch-divisions are presented as irregular progressions from high to low, each division contained in a specific bandwidth, while the duration-progression is regular. Furthermore, this presentation suggests a specific acoustic awareness by Messiaen (a perspective, the young Pierre Boulez will continue to connect only with Varèse) since by 'verticalising' each division a structure results in which the lowest values are the longest and the highest the shortest, a clear analogy to the sound-spectrum of an harmonic sound. — 1948 was also the year of the first presentation of the initial realisations of musique concrète by Pierre Schaeffer.

The following considerations are not intended as an analysis of the *Mode* but as an attempt to clarify why Boulez was interested in the first pitch-division as starting point for his *Structures*-project beyond the anecdotal homage to his teacher. Indeed, as Robert Piencikowski showed more than twenty years ago, division I is structured by tritone-relations: the first two pitches (E-flat/D) are immediately transposed a tritone down (A/A-flat); this same relationship can be observed for the next three pitches (G/F-sharp/E become C-sharp/C/B-flat) as well as for the last pair (F becomes B). Similar pecularities appear in division III: the first three pitches are a transposition two octaves down of the beginning of division I; other tritones appear here in strict succession (in the mode, which does not imply that it will necessarily be so in the music), F-sharp/C, F/B, E/B-flat. Messiaen used precisely his modal technique (where he was not constrained by a specific order as would have been the case in a theme-based or serial organization) to emphasize more or less these relationships, whether they are 'hidden' as in division I or explicit as in division III.

Let us take the beginning of the composition: in bars 1–3, Messiaen gives the listener the characteristic highest 'motive' completely, that is to say the four first pitches in the order of the mode, the successive intervals being (in interval-classes) 1–5–1. The subjacent relationships by the tritone (between E-flat/A and D/A-flat) are not translated into an immediate succession at the foreground-level: this harmonic connection remains in the 'middleground'. But in bar 2, Messiaen juxtaposes E and B-flat in the upper part, immediately echoed by the inversion B-flat to E in the middle part (i.e. division II, where tritones, as far as I can see, do not have the same structural function). Shortly after, at bars 8–10, the lower part emphasizes *ff* the pitch-classes E-flat, D and A-flat, highlighting a tritone separated by an octave and completing (from the point of view of pitch-class-relationships) the reduced beginning of the initial motive of division I that appears in the next bar. At the first appearance of the low C-sharp (the lowest note of the composition, whose occurences in a certain sense punctuate the whole composition) in bar 28, there is a very interesting treatment of the tritones in division I. At first (bars 29–30), there is a modal succession restricted to ic1 and ic4 relations (each pitch considered as a pc): the characteristic beginning reduced to two notes, E-flat and D, followed by B and B-flat. In bars 31–33 a kind of repetition of this figure occurs, enlarged by interpolated tritone relationships: D followed by A-flat, B followed by F before B-flat is finally played.

In Messiaen's modal universe, highlighting one or the other harmonic relationship is rather easy, since the composer has a total freedom with relation to the order of succession of the elements. His freedom was here even enhanced since the *Mode* is based on single objects with an all-parametric identity, and since Messiaen considered the other dimensions (duration, dynamic and attack) apparently not designed to build specific relationships. Since Messiaen left aside his former rhythms, his way of composing changed here profoundly: it really became the handling of predefined 'sound-objects', which were no longer at the disposal of the composer for contextual adaptation through modification (altering of duration, register etc.). The restrictions Messiaen imposed on himself were even stronger here than Schaeffer's submission to the recorded sounds in his first noise-studies.

The problem of revealing at the surface more or less hidden but structurally important features is much more problematic in serial music. The two solutions are either to leave the serial ordering aside at certain moments (and then it is legitimate to ask why even adopt the serial technique?), or to reflect on the system's impact on the surface and to find some kind of equilibrium between both these levels (or at least one or the other even exceptional situation where the reciprocal determination of structure and surface can be made obvious to an attentive listener).

* * *

It was also in 1948 that Boulez published his first article, 'Propositions'. He identified two strains in the music of the first half of the century (they later became the major axes for most of the historiography concerning this period): Schoenberg, for his research in the realm of pitch, and Stravinsky, for his explorations in the domain of rhythm (the latter was extended by Messiaen). Boulez chose atonality as the basic reference point and considered the dodecaphonic perspective of Schoenberg as being the point of departure for a really new musical language. Since he wanted to transgress the contradictions of the music of the first half of the century by an original synthesis, he concluded his article by advocating the necessity for an 'atonal rhythm' to combine with the principle of the series (which Schoenberg invented, but did not — according to Boulez — understand its full implications). In 1949, John Cage was in Paris, and a profound exchange began between the two composers who were subsequently considered as the two poles of contemporary music. At that time, they obviously shared many ideas, and Boulez discovered in Cage's music a way of constructing relationships between the micro- and macro-level for which there was no example in European music so far. Furthermore, there seemed to be a strange parallelism between Messiaen's thoughts on independent sound-dimensions and Cage's compositional method since the thirties. (The separation of acoustic dimensions was also the basis for the first electric instruments that had been built since the late twenties, different technical means being responsible for each of these aspects in the resulting sound.) It took Boulez a few years to come to the synthesis to which he aspired and which he fully realized in his *Structures*-project.

It is well known, that the point of departure of what will become the first book of *Structures* is the division I of Messiaen's *Mode*. Boulez transformed this given structure into a row and developed a fully serial project on this basis. At first, he was concerned with systematising the pitch-dimension. Indeed, in the scores of the composers of the Viennese School, there did not seem to be a need to relate the basic row itself and its treatment on larger scales, beginning with the order of succession of the row's transpositions. So Boulez, as explained in 'Eventuellement…' (1952), organized his row-table by transposing the basic series according to its own hierarchy: the second form begins its transposition on pitch two of the row; the third form on pitch three etc. (According to a recent, private report by Michel Fano, this also seems to be the way Messiaen presented the row table in his analysis of Alban Berg's *Lyric Suite* in his teaching.) The complete row-table shows peculiarities already identified by Piencikowski: complementarities between adjacent row-forms around the structuring tritones. Boulez exploits these complementarities at the foreground level of *Structure Ia* in the first section of the second part. As shown by Piencikowski, the pitch-rows as well as the duration-rows are in parallel tritone relations: this is the reason why at certain places in this section, the tritone E-flat/A is played as a simultaneous event (as in the harp's part of Anton Webern's *Symphony* op. 21, beginning of the first movement) in both piano parts. [example 2] Since each pitch-row-form is linked to a duration-row-form (which always uses all twelve chromatic duration-values), there is a strict synchronisation of the beginnings and endings of all the rows in these two dimensions. Dynamics and articulation are used to unify the different objects of one row-strain as shown already in late fifties in the piece's first analyses (by György Ligeti and Marc Wilkinson both published in 1958 — it is probable that Karlheinz Stockhausen also analysed it this way in his Darmstadt seminars in 1957).

*Example 2.*

In *Structure Ic*, the next movement of the cycle from the point of view of compositional chronology (completed after Boulez's experiments in Schaeffer's studio at the Paris radio station), Boulez began to introduce flexibility in the relationship between pitch-rows and duration-rows, since the latter could either consist in a complete sequence of the twelve chromatic duration-values or in a periodic presentation of the successive pitches of a row according to the first value only of the selected duration-row. The practical result is that the different pitch-rows are played at variable speeds, distinguishing furthermore between regular and statistical (i.e. serial) repartition of the events of one row-strain. At the beginning of the movement, this is immediately obvious [example 3]: in Piano I, Boulez graphically displays one row-form by linking all its notes, each playing a semiquaver (bars 1–3); the two other voices also evolve in regular steps, but slower (by steps of 6 and 9 demisemiquavers). The fourth row-form to appear (middle voice from bar 4 onward) presents a different duration for each. In Piano II, the situation is similar (12 and 8 demisemiquaversas regular steps for the outer voices while the middle voice displays all chromatic values).

*Example 3.*

The situation becomes far more complicated in *Structure Ib*, where Boulez constantly invents new strategies to translate numbers and number-groupings into specific *rhythmic groups*. These rhythmic groups are not identical to Messiaen's rhythms (even if the latter consisted of grouped durations): in Boulez's *Structure Ib*, the grouping structure is revealed by strong identities, whether in the form of regular rhythmic subdivisions or in the form of a sequence of pitches linked together through an identical intensity- or articulation-level. A simple look at the score is sufficient to understand the flexibility (and thus the freedom) Boulez has gained in his serial approach.

*Le Marteau sans maître* is known for its organization according to three interwoven cycles, each cycle being based on a different serial technique, a different way of constructing hierarchies starting from the same basic-row. These techniques were explained by Boulez as early as 1954 in his article '… auprès et au loin.'. Three of the four serial techniques Boulez revealed (the first one concerns *Structures*, the other three *Marteau*) focus so strongly on pitch problems (transposition of a basic-row in terms of pitch-classes; creation of harmonic entities through 'sound multiplication'; vertical control through serial means), that the question of rhythm was approached only incidentally. As for the third technique, Boulez stressed immediately the close relationship between the dimensions of pitch and rhythm and gave the latter even a structural priority. Let us consider two examples showing divergent strategies and different listening perspectives — such a polarisation being stressed by Boulez himself in his analysis of Stravinsky's *The Rite* written between 1951 and 1953 ('Stravinsky demeure'): the opposition between subdivided global values ('Introduction' of *The Rite*) and additive rhythms ('Danse sacrale').

In the cycle '*L'Artisanat furieux*', Boulez used 'sound blocs' with variable density and with non-oriented development of their constituents (that is to say no preestablished ordering of the pitches composing a complex in the case of their horizontal presentation, for example, by a solo-instrument such as the flute in the third movement). The rhythmic equivalent of these sound blocs, as suggested already in the former article 'Eventuellement ...' (1952), are *rhythmic cells* of variable density. The choice of the term 'cell' instead of Messiaen's 'rhythm' is to be understood on the basis of a certain degree of abstraction whereas Messiaen's rhythms were concrete entities: from Boulez's perspective, a cell is defined only by the number of principal attacks (here: from one to four), not by specific durational relationships between the values of a cell nor by the relationship between total cell-durations from one to the other. There is no given first rhythm, no basic *personnage*. From the point of view of coherence in Boulez's serial system, this is not only sufficient (there is a strong relationship between the densities of the rhythmic cells and the grouping of pitches on the level of the basic row for the derivation of the sound blocs) but also necessary, since he is looking for a maximum degree of flexibility through which the composer would be able to express himself freely on a globally controlled canvas. And this flexibility has to exist on all levels, each level operating in its own universe. The following example is relatively simple but allows on the one hand to understand the basis of Boulez's approach in this cycle, and contains on the other hand sufficient ad hoc-solutions to demonstrate the flexibility the composer was looking for.

In the introductory sequence of movement III, played by the flute [example 4b], five sound blocs are melodically developed in time according to five rhythmic cells (each cell giving rise to a bar). The compositional problem Boulez has to negotiate constantly is the relationship between the density of the blocs (here:

7–9–6–4–8) and the number of attacks in a cell (here: 1–2–4–2–3). Since, taken as one to one relationships, the bloc-densities are always superior to the cell-densities, there is no need for a local arrangement and the question for Boulez was how to develop the sound-blocs in time so as to assure his aesthetic aspiration of flexibility to also determine the musical surface and thus the perception of his music. Flexibility was translated in terms of 'no perceptible tempo' but only constantly and irregularly fluctuating movement. On an initial level, Boulez chose values for the successive cells that constantly alter the reference duration (dotted crotchet, minim, crotchet triplet, dotted quaver, crotchet) and thus the 'felt tempo'; on a second level, he adopted two distinct solutions to distribute the 'exceeding' pitches on the attacks he has at his disposal: 1) the regular subdivision of an attack (semiquaver septuplet in bar 1, semiquaver quintuplet on the first beat and two quavers on the last beat of bar 5 — this technique corresponds to Messiaen's *monnayage*); 2) the irregular distribution of groups of 'little notes' (appogiaturas) preceeding a principal attack of a cell (5[4]–2–1–1–0–0–2 in bars 2–4). In this case, the distribution of the two solutions suggests a symmetric arrangement, but this suggestion is purely graphic: by listening to a performance of the piece, it is impossible to decide exactly which notation had been used, nor does it seem desirable to ask performers to translate the different notations into two differentiated classes of figuration. What is clearly heard finally is an absence of pulse, or a constantly changing pulse (in bar 3 for example, there is a slight chance of hearing the pulse since the first of the four values is not altered by a ligatura and the single little notes at the beginning of the two first attacks are not strong perturbations). Furthermore, there are groups of sounds that are played so fast, that they merge into a single complex entity. From this point of view, we could come to a more convincing description of a perceptible (even if incomplete) symmetry of compounded sound phenomena in terms of attack (with variable density) and sustain, since the perceived density of the attacks evolves as follows: 6–4–2–1–1–2–4.

The first vocal line [example 4c] allows us to focus on another issue. The bloc-densities (6–3–2–6–3) present a problem when connected to the cell-densities (2–4–2–3–1) since the second bloc contains only three pitches, which is insufficient to realize the required four attacks. Since, furthermore, there is a common pitch between the blocs 2 and 3, Boulez unifies both blocs into one single unit and splits the following fourth bloc (six pitches) to realise the next two cells (a total of five attacks), and thus to redress synchronicity between the two determinations. In the rhythmic realisation itself, Boulez left the context of periodicity inside the cells since from this second section on, irregular proportions between cell-durations occur beside the initial regularity, thus increasing through a supplementary means the fluidity of time.

*Example 4.*

By contrast, the cycle '*Bourreaux de solitude*' is clearly pulsatory. While the changes of tempo-feeling were fluid in '*L'Artisanat furieux*', Boulez juxtaposed here sections with identifiable tempi changing by discrete steps from one section to another. The determinations for durations and dynamics conform to the former stage of *Structures*, that is to say, multiplication of a basic unit by values from 1 to 12 and 12 discrete degrees of intensity (six dynamic-pairs internally differentiated by means of articulation). These two levels and a grid of twelve entrance-points were connected by Boulez to determine the basic structure of this cycle. As he wrote in '… auprès et au loin.', the pitch domain served now to vary this horizontal regularity by constantly changing vertical densities at each entrance-point. The specific serial technique of deriving the pitch-structures resulted in a 12x12 table, where horizontally and vertically, each box indicated a specific density, varying irregularly from 0 to 4. Empty boxes were realised through interventions of the untuned percussion instruments, so that the lack is only relative to pitch but not to rhythm.

In the first bar of movement VI, the basic unit is a semiquaver. On each semiquaver of the bar a sound-event occurs, be it a percussion-sound or one or more variously sustained pitches: only the attacks determine the perception of the basic pulse, whereas the variable duration has effects on the inner transformation of the more global sound-texture. At the beginning of bar 2, the felt tempo changes to half the tempo, since the unit regulating the entrance-points changes suddenly to an quaver. The beginning of the third row-form is slightly anticipated: instead of beginning at bar 4, Boulez fused both row-forms by the common pair B-flat/D (vibraphone and guitar belong to the second row-form while xylorimba and viola belong to the third one, as does the supplementary anticipation of the A in the flute). The felt-tempo is again the initial one, with the semiquaver as the pulse. This structure of three grouped rows ends with a 'resonance-bar' of 5/16. The latter duration is simply the result of the remaining durations to be completed, since at bar 6 a new group of three rows begins, now alternating quaver triplets and quavers as the basic pulse. The temporal strategy here is thus a clear pulse-feeling changing from section to section with measured (but not pulsating) resonances at the end of a structure grouping a certain number of row-forms.

\* \* \*

Stockhausen's theory of musical time as formulated around 1955 has often been reduced to the question of the chromatic scale of tempi. Even if this issue was important enough to be highlighted, its full meaning is significant only in the context of the instrumental pieces that Stockhausen began at the same time as *Gesang der Jünglinge*, that is to say, *Zeitmaße* and *Gruppen*. So what were the reasons for developing such a tool, and was it more than a goal in itself?

To begin, we must briefly recapitulate the necessity for Stockhausen of his chosen solution in the wider context of serial thinking. As Stockhausen demonstrated in '… wie die Zeit vergeht …' (1957), considering a series in terms of proportions (intervals) instead of simply regarding it as a sequence of objects, implies a reconsideration of the formerly adopted solutions for chromaticism in the domain of durations. The only solution is to work with variable speeds — a possibility technically already suggested by the *phonogène* in Schaeffer's studio in Paris. But what is needed to *perceive* tempi relations? A tempo is expressed through metric relations, not through durational relations. That is why Stockhausen connected the idea of chromatic tempi with group-structures, so that the basic pulse of a corresponding tempo might be perceived through repetition. Stockhausen thus had to reflect on periodicity, a feature stylistically considered as problematic in serial music (this questions was, for example, very prominent in the correspondence between Boulez and Henri Pousseur around 1952, the latter considering every kind of regularity and periodicity as a submission under the former laws of tonality).

The reason to enlarge the conception of serial music to encompass periodicity was given by the starting points of *Gesang der Jünglinge* as well as of *Gruppen*. In both cases, Stockhausen wanted to include sounds like the sung voice in *Gesang* and the orchestral instruments with definite pitch in *Gruppen*. Now the sung voice and these instruments, according to the knowledge of acoustics at the middle of the twentieth century, are precisely characterised by harmonic timbres, and the composer has no possibility of modifying such data. The use of sounds with periodic micro-level-characteristics necessarily led to consequences concerning the way of considering these projects as a whole. During his experiments in the electronic studio (but also in Meyer-Eppler's teaching at Bonn University) Stockhausen was confronted with the idea of the physical time continuum, which is divided into specific areas (duration, pitch, timbre) only by our perception. Stockhausen's serial conception led him to translate the qualities he could observe in his material on certain levels to other ones, which no longer were given by the material itself but decisions of the composer relative to his compositional method. The coherence of the aesthetic project thus resulted not from a simple transfer of a certain logic deduced from one dimension to the others, but from taking into account all combined basic constraints. In Stockhausen's time continuum, timbre and pitch are two adjacent domains. Timbre is considered as given 'by nature' and conforms to the criterion of periodicity, harmonicity; pitch-organization, on the other hand, was fully chromatic (a feature inherited by Webern). To create a specific sense of coherence, he transferred the characteristics of this domain-couple (vertically harmonic, horizontally chromatic) towards the other time-domains that are immediately perceptible: duration, meter (understood as grouping of durations) and different levels of form-building. This gives rise to the following subdivision of collective characteristics:

| overall group relations— formal plan | group relations (relative duration) | meter | duration | pitch | timbre |
|---|---|---|---|---|---|
| overall chromaticism of the group-relations | harmonic proportions between successive groups | chromatic tempi | harmonic time spectra | chromaticism | harmonic sound-spectra of the instruments |
| 12 successive 12-tone-rows governing the overall form | durations of the groups in terms of harmonic proportions | a 12-tone-row governs the time-relations | structuration of a basic duration through layers of entire subdivisions | stylistic serial constraint | physical constraint |

*Example 5: Relations of the couple harmonicism-chromatism over the complete time continuum.*

The first realisation of this new conception was in the final part of *Zeitmaße* (a composition Stockhausen coincidentally began in August 1955). Indeed, in the sketches of *Gruppen*, besides the search for specific proportionalities for the time-plan of the orchestra piece, one registered twelve-tone-row enlarged by harmonic proportions occurs between the successive pitches as well as tempo-indications. This row is revealed to be the basis of the final part of *Zeitmaße*, consisting of twelve sections (one for each pitch of the row) differentiated by their tempi, their total duration and a variable treatment of vertical density (the density being controlled through a series of modulo 5, since there are five instruments involved in this composition). To relate this sketch [example 6] to the score, three modifications need to be taken into account: 1) the tempi differ slightly from the scale published by Stockhausen in his article and which he also adopted for the published score; 2) the tempo-indications of 66 and 80 have been exchanged (without any consequences on the other levels) to emphasize the global gesture of extinction at the end of the composition; 3) the metric unit has been doubled.

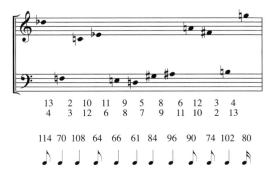

*Example 6.*

The tempi reflect the chromatic organisation of the row; the pitches' registration has consequences for the basic-duration (i.e. the metric unit), here with a repartition on three different time-octaves (crotchet, quaver, semiquaver for the final g); the harmonic proportions are translated into the global duration of each section, the number of metric units — their grouping — resulting from the denominators of the proportions (except for the first section, the duration of which is deduced from the numerator since this section is not linked to a former event by such a proportion). Since the employed row is symmetrical, this reading of the proportions results in a double occurence of numeral 13 while numeral 5 is omitted. That is why Stockhausen realised a certain interaction between these two numerals in the final section: its global duration is of fourteen units (the slight stretching is to avoid the last sound to be played on a down-beat, which would usually result in a stress, and would be completely against the present gesture of a progressive 'fade-out') and only the first five basic-durations continue to be determined by the above mentioned density-modification. After this serially coherent group of five values follow four 'adieux' each consisting of a sustained tone preceded by respectively 2–3–1–0 appogiaturas.

In *Gruppen*, besides the extension of a group which is, like in *Zeitmaße*, deduced from the interval-proportions between successive units, the maximal number of layers for the harmonic subdivision of a basic-duration ('time-spectrum') is also determined by these numerals. The horizontal and vertical dimensions are thus interdependent: the longer a group, the finer the subdivision of the basic durational unit. The inner repartition is again serial, fluctuating irregularly between the minimum of one single rhythmic harmonic subdivision to the maximum given the group's extension. Furthermore, since the orchestra is subdivided into three independent parts, each under a specific conductor, it was now possible to give to both terms of the proportion a significance relevant for the time-shaping of the composition. Indeed, Stockhausen worked here with two distinct time-determinations, the first being the interval of entrance ('Einsatzabstand') between successive events (derived from the numerator of the proportion), the second the proper duration of each event (derived from the denominator). If a numerator is inferior to the denominator of the preceeding proportion, the orchestras will overlap; if the numerator is superior, there will be a silence between two adjacent structures. (Further details are evident from the examples 16 and 17 given by Misch, 1998, showing the time-organization for the beginning of the composition.)

While in *Zeitmaße* the vertical density depended on the number of instruments and the basic-durations limited to the mid-range, the expansion of the time-scale in *Gruppen* had other specific implications. For obvious practical reasons, Stockhausen limited the shortest playable value to about 1/16th of a second (the coincidence with the threshold between rhythm- and pitch-perception is certainly significant). The consequence of this further 'material constraint', was that for certain long groups with short basic-durations, all the harmonic layers might not be playable if maintained according to the primary logic of time-spectra.

Stockhausen thus used a 'time-filter'-device according to which the requested thirteen subdivisions per basic-duration will be accessible only for basic-durations superior or equal to a whole note; for a minim, the subdivisions will be restricted to a maximum of 12; for a crotchet, to 8; for a quaver, to 4; and finally for a semiquaver to 2. The loss of harmonic subdivisions nevertheless does not affect the vertical density, since the filtering-device does not simply 'cut-off' the values which are too short but acts by simplifying them to possible ones. Two short examples [example 7]. In group 12 in orchestra II, the reference proportion of 5:12 should result in a global duration of 12 quarters and the basic duration should be subdivided into a maximum of twelve layers (this is shown in example 7a). But since the filter-device restricts the possible values for a basic-duration of a quarter to a maximum of 8 levels, Stockhausen modified the subdivisions by adopting a simplification criterion that seems to be 'division by 2 or 3' (12 becomes a supplementary layer of 6, 10 of 5, 9 of 3 — 11 as prime-number is simplified into a second layer of 7); since layer 8 had to appear only once according to the initial determination, Stockhausen filtered this value as well (see example 7b). In group 36 in orchestra II, the situation is even more complex since the basic-duration is a semiquaver, and thus all the playable values will be either semiquavers or demisemiquavers. The corresponding sketch by Stockhausen can be reconstructed as a sequence of different stages. Example 7c shows the basic version, wherein Stockhausen replaced the numeral 5 by 6 (such changes occur systematically in the sketches for all series with an odd density); example 7d shows the repartition once the filter-device is applied;

group 12

**a**

| 12 | 8 | 1 | 10 | 9 | 11 | 5 | 3 | 4 | 7 | 2 | 6 |
|---|---|---|---|---|---|---|---|---|---|---|---|
| 12 | 12 |  | 12 | 12 | 12 | 12 |  |  | 12 |  | 12 |
| 11 | 11 |  | 11 | 11 | 11 |  |  |  |  |  |  |
| 10 | 10 |  | 10 | 10 | 10 | 10 |  | 10 | 10 |  | 10 |
| 9 | 9 |  | 9 | 9 | 9 | 9 | 9 | 9 | 9 | 9 | 9 |
| 8 |  |  |  |  |  |  |  |  |  |  |  |
| 7 |  |  |  | 7 |  |  |  |  |  |  |  |
| 6 | 6 | 6 | 6 | 6 | 6 | 6 | 6 | 6 | 6 | 6 | 6 |
| 5 |  | 5 |  | 5 |  |  |  |  |  |  |  |
| 4 | 4 |  | 4 | 4 | 4 |  |  |  | 4 |  | 4 |
| 3 |  |  | 3 | 3 | 3 |  |  |  |  |  |  |
| 2 | 2 |  | 2 | 2 | 2 |  |  |  | 2 |  |  |
| 1 | 1 |  | 1 | 1 | 1 | 1 | 1 | 1 | 1 |  | 1 |

**b**

| 12 | 8 | 1 | 10 | 9 | 11 | 5 | 3 | 4 | 7 | 2 | 6 |
|---|---|---|---|---|---|---|---|---|---|---|---|
|  |  |  |  |  |  |  |  |  |  |  |  |
|  |  |  |  |  |  |  |  |  |  |  |  |
|  |  |  |  |  |  |  |  |  |  |  |  |
|  |  |  |  |  |  |  |  |  |  |  |  |
|  |  |  |  |  |  |  |  |  |  |  |  |
| $7^2$ |  |  |  | $7^2$ |  |  |  |  |  |  |  |
| $6^2$ | $6^3$ | 6 | $6^2$ | $6^2$ | $6^2$ | $6^3$ | $6^2$ | $6^2$ | $6^3$ | $6^2$ | $6^3$ |
| $5^2$ |  |  | $5^2$ | $5^2$ |  |  |  |  |  |  |  |
| $4^2$ | 4 |  | 4 | $4^2$ | 4 |  |  |  | 4 |  | $4^2$ |
| $3^2$ |  |  | $3^2$ | $3^2$ | $3^2$ |  |  |  |  |  |  |
| 2 | $2^2$ |  | 2 | 2 | 2 |  |  |  |  | $2^2$ |  |
| 1 | $1^2$ |  | $1^2$ | $1^2$ | 1 | $1^2$ | 1 | $1^2$ | 1 |  | 1 |

groupe 36

**c**

| 4 | 6 | 3 | 1 | 2 |
|---|---|---|---|---|
| 6 | 6 |  |  |  |
| 4 | 4 | 4 | 4 | 4 |
| 3 | 3 | 3 |  | 3 |
|  | 2 |  |  |  |
| 1 | 1 | 1 |  |  |

**d**

| 4 | 6 | 3 | 1 | 2 |
|---|---|---|---|---|
|  |  |  |  |  |
|  |  |  |  |  |
|  |  |  |  |  |
|  | $2^3$ |  |  | 2 |
| $1^4$ | $1^2$ | $1^3$ |  | 1 |

example 7e shows the rhythmic repartition adopted in the sketches while 7f transcribes the score. Two exceptional features need further comment. From the first to the second basic-duration, the four expressed basic-durations were expected to be prolonged onto the second basic-duration, resulting in four quavers. In the score, only two such values appear: in the piccolo-clarinet (which is an 'out of structure'-addition linked to another criterion of the piece, i.e. the repartition of specific harmonic fields whose predominant interval is always announced by this instrument) and in the drums, while vibraphone and guitar display a subdivision into two 32nd notes (which can be explained due to the overlapping with group 35 whose pitch-bandwith is also taken over for this first basic duration). The second and third basic-durations conform to the rhythmical sketch and express the specific bandwith in the pitch domain. The second exception occurs on the fourth basic-duration: indeed, Stockhausen's sketch does not show

how to reduce the numeral 4; an interpretation might be that he adopts the subdivision 2 (demisemiquavers) and that he writes an exceptional rhythm (demisemiquaverfollowed by dotted semiquaver, i.e. 1+3 demisemiquavers) to refer to the numeral 4 that should have been the value continuously present throughout this group.

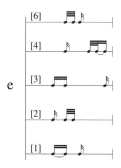

*Example 7.*

Other exceptional features attest how Stockhausen progressively expanded his rhythmic considerations beyond the chromaticism of the twelve tempi distributed over approximately 6 octaves. In the groups 157 (orchestra II) to 167, which constitute section XII of Stockhausen's overall plan for the 'character-repartition', the basic-durations are expressed by only one harmonic subdivision at a time. This allows a kind of 'finer modulation' of the discrete steps of the chromatic tempi-scale and tends to a dissolution of these discrete elements in a quasi continuum. Such a continuum becomes then the major time-shaping-feature in the three soli Stockhausen inserted into this structural framework, each solo concluding one structural section by emphasizing once more the predominant timbre-characterisations of the former section. The reference tempo in the inserted soli is 60 or a multiple of it, and the continuous sliding between different register positions of this reference tempo (either by change of the proper tempo-indication, for instance, from 60 per unit to 120 for this same unit, or by change of the unit's duration, for instance, from crotchet to quaver) joins all the chromatic steps into a tempo-continuum which

is equivalent to the glissando in the pitch-domain. This latter characteristic is almost non-existent in this score, but in at least one place, in group 6, it reflects precisely Stockhausen's intention also to transgress the limitations of chromaticism in the domain of pitch. To fully understand the significance of the glissandi in group 6, one has to go back to the first manuscript full-score of *Gruppen*. At this point in the composition's genesis, the score was intended for three 'double' orchestras: three orchestras playing on stage and three other ones being prerecorded and 'adjusted' in the studio. There was a double purpose. On the one hand, Stockhausen had in mind the confrontation between fixed tempi and mobile tempi — something he had worked out on a smaller level in *Zeitmaße* with the parts added to the score between January and June 1956 (since a first version of the piece had been recorded and broadcasted on Cologne Radio in January 1956). *Gruppen* was planned as being the *summa summarum* of all Stockhausen's research, and in the sketches there are suggestions which even appear to integrate possibilities of aleatoric succession of predetermined sections into this project, which would have been a continuation of *Klavierstück XI*, composed in the summer of 1956. On the other hand, each group was (beyond all the rhythmic features that have been described here) individualised by a specific pitch-treatment, since Stockhausen determined for each group a frequency-bandwith, within which a group had to operate and to display statistically more or less clearly oriented movements (ascending or descending tendency according to the reference-pitch of the next group, in order to have an inner articulation that would compensate for the non-existing transitions between the groups). For group 6, the pitch-structure gave the indication of a minor third as bandwith: in his first full-score, Stockhausen attributed this group to one of the prerecorded orchestras, and composed a microtonal cluster of twelve steps within this boundary of the minor third. After cancelling the idea of the prerecorded orchestras, he had to redesign this group for the orchestra on stage and chose the glissandi as symbols for the finer scales also in the domain of pitch.

To conclude this panorama, one last observation on *Gruppen* and *Zeitmaße*. Up to now, my description was limited to the temporal framework of the time-spectra. But Stockhausen really 'sculpted' these spectra in terms of specific evolutions in time, alluding to the shape of a sound in time with its characteristic parts of attack, sustain and decay. That is why, for instance, the first group of the composition (which is preceeded by a cluster enunciating precisely the frequency bandwith that will be displayed 'stretched' through the time during all the ten basic-durations of group 1) begins progressively (the two last subdivisions of each rhythmic harmonic symbolising the attack from longer to shorter values), and suddenly stops on basic-duration 2 with a clear cut-off of all harmonics before a melodic resonance on basic-duration 3 with the solo-violin, to begin a new three-units-long texture with progressive entries from long to short values and an extinction in basic-duration 6 which filters from the extremities to the centre, before the last four basic-durations display a final growth and descent of this sound in time. In this group, all the values of subdivision of the harmonics are expressed, the missing elements being subjected precisely to the global evolution in time with attacks and decays. From the middle of group 4 on, Stockhausen used tied values, the basic periodicity of an harmonic being slightly altered but not yet becoming imperceptible. In the center of group 7 (which is a filled-in silence, the structural groups being number 6 and number 9), silences of irregular value take the place of the tied values, and finally (beginning with group 11 in orchestra III), the horizontal articulation of each present rhythmic harmonic subdivision becomes completely statistic (i.e. that all grouping values from 1 to a maximum are used but in a statistic (non-ordered) repartition. The notion of statistic is furthermore of great importance, since it is the link towards noise — which is generally described as statistic repartition of frequencies). This last effect which brings the horizontal rhythmic articulation closest to 'noise' is controlled by means of the series, this tool enabling the composer to avoid perceptible repetitions (this is very clear in the parts of piccolo-clarinet and solo-violin I,1 in group 12). Clearly, Stockhausen had in mind the scale of his orchestral timbres with sustained sound of definite pitch, percussion (and thus more or less staccato) sounds with definite pitch and finally percussion sounds of indefinite pitch. This spectral richness had to be translated also to the slower time-domains, and the horizontal articulation of each rhythmic harmonic seemed to the composer an appropriate solution.

Let us from this point of the reflection now switch to the inserted parts of *Zeitmaße*, where the different instruments evolve independently one from the other: certain instruments playing more or less fixed tempi (either a certain metronomic indication or suggestions like 'as slow/fast as possible') while others have to accelerate or decelerate very quickly — according to a ratio of 1:4 between the beginning and the end of a given passage. These continuous time-curves have the effect, since the different instruments play harmonic subdivisions of basic-units, of enlarging the reference-system by a new specificity, which is a non regular reference-pulse for the harmonic subdivisions. Retranslated according to the sound-model that is at the basis of Stockhausen's compositional thinking at that moment of his carreer, this implies a further step on the scale of irregularities inside a domain until expressed by a more or less recognisable pulse.

Even if the composer did not imagine such a solution at the moment when he started his project and defined its basic structural laws, this new, 'discovered' situation appears clearly as an unexpected but nevertheless coherent expansion of the basic system more than as a withdrawal of the former strictness to celebrate subjective freedom. If there is subjective freedom in serial music (and there is!), it is rooted in the open-minded attitude of these composers. A categorical contrast between strict and free composition does not exist any more in this music than in the music of the Viennese classic period (see Schenker). Contrast is too simple a concept to conform to serial thinking, whose major device has always been 'mediation'.

SOURCES

The sketches relative to the discussed compositions of Boulez and Stockhausen, as well as their correspondence, have been consulted at the Paul Sacher Foundation in Basel.

BIBLIOGRAPHY

- Pierre Boulez, *Relevés d'apprenti*, Paris, Seuil, 1966 [contains 'Propositions', 'Eventuellement …', 'Stravinsky demeure' and '… auprès et au loin.'].
- Pascal Decroupet (ed.), *Pierre Boulez : Le Marteau sans maître (1952-55). Fac-similé de l'épure et de la première mise au net / Facsimile of the draft score and the first fair copy of the full score*, A Publication of the Paul Sacher Foundation, Mainz, Schott, 2005.
- Pascal Decroupet and Jean-Louis Leleu, '«Penser sensiblement la musique»: production et description du matériau harmonique dans le troisième mouvement du *Marteau sans maître*', in: *Pierre Boulez: techniques d'écriture et enjeux esthétiques*, Jean-Louis Leleu and Pascal Decroupet (eds), Genève, Contrechamps, 2006, pp. 177-215.
- György Ligeti, 'Pierre Boulez. Entscheidung und Automatik in der Structure Ia', in: *die Reihe* 4 (1958), pp. 38-63; English edition 1960, pp. 36-62.
- Olivier Messiaen, *Technique de mon langage musical*, Paris, Leduc, 1944; English version translated by John Satterfield, 1956.
- Imke Misch, 'On the Serial Shaping of Stockhausen's *Gruppen für 3 Orchester*', in: *Perspectives of New Music* 36/1 (1998), pp. 143-187.
- ――――――, *Zur Kompositionstechnik Karlheinz Stockhausens: GRUPPEN für 3 Orchester (1955-57)*, Saarbrücken, Pfau, 1999.
- Robert Piencikowski, 'Nature morte avec guitare', in: *Pierre Boulez. Eine Festschrift zum 60. Geburtstag am 26. März 1985*, ed. by Josef Häusler, Vienna, Universal Edition, 1985, pp. 66-81.
- Marc Wilkinson, 'Pierre Boulez' "Structure Ia". Bemerkungen zur Zwölfton-Technik', in: *Gravesaner Blätter* 4/10 (1958), pp. 12-18; Examples, pp. 19-22; English text, pp. 23-29.
- Stockhausen Karlheinz, '… wie die Zeit vergeht …', in: *Texte*, vol. 1, Cologne, DuMont, 1963, pp. 99-139.

# TIME IS TIME:
## TEMPORAL SIGNIFICATION IN MUSIC

*Bruce Brubaker*

PART ONE

O' O"

*Illustration 1: Clock at the Bristol Corn Exchange.*

John Cage might have said, "Time is time," as he did say, "Sounds are sounds." Of course, what he really said is: "Before studying music, men are men and sounds are sounds..." [1] He was riffing on what he said Daisetz Teitaro Suzuki said:

> Dr. Suzuki said: "Before studying Zen, men are men and mountains are mountains. While studying Zen things become

---

1. John Cage, "Juilliard Lecture", *A Year From Monday*, Middletown, Connecticut 1967, p. 96.

95

confused: one doesn't know exactly what is what and which is which. After studying Zen, men are men and mountains are mountains."[2]

So, as Jacques Lacan said, on television: "I always speak the truth. Never the whole truth, because there's no way to say it all..."[3] Lacan doesn't put it this way, but — it's a matter of time.

I have sometimes said, "Music is the sound of time passing." But, what do we signify with such words? ..."time passing"...? I lost track of time...? I wasted time ... ran out of time ... saved some time...? It's *about time*! That was timely. Take your time. Be sure to allow enough time. Since time immemorial. (Ah, we need "memory"... to have time.) We say, "He learned to tell time." We also say: "Time will tell."

Time's up!

Time flies!

Time flies — *tempus fugit.*

**Tempus fugit** is a <u>Latin</u> expression meaning "time flees", more commonly translated as "time flies". It is frequently used as an inscription on clocks. The expression was first used in the verse *Georgica* written by the Roman poet Virgil: *Sed fugit interea fugit irreparabile tempus* ... It is the title of a composition by the ... rock group Yes, from the 1980 album *Drama*. Tempus Fugit is the title of a song by... Miles Davis ... Also the title of a famous composition *Tempus Fugue-It* ... by the jazz pianist Bud Powell.[4]

So, the Romans had "tempus" — the Latin word for time. Giving us in English, and perhaps indirectly, "temporal" and "temporary."

---

2. Ibid., pp. 95–96.
3. Jacques Lacan, *Television: a challenge to the establishment* [*Télévision*, 1974], (trans.) Denis Hollier, Rosalind Krauss, and Annette Michelson, New York 1990, p. 3.
4. from the entry "Tempus fugit", in: *Wikipedia, the free encyclopedia,* http://en.wikipedia. org/wiki/Tempus_fugit accessed 3 March 2007.

In French, there's "temps", a word commonly signifying time; "Le temps fait beau," is a description of good weather. In Greek, "chronos" is the basic word for time.

In Greek mythology, **Chronos** (Χρόνος in Greek) in pre-Socratic philosophical works is said to be the personification of time. He emerged from the primordial Chaos.[5]

(So, before time, chaos.)

He was depicted in Greco-Roman mosaics as a man turning the zodiac wheel. Often the figure is named Aeon (Eternal Time), a common alternate name for the god... Some of the current English words which show a tie to khronos/**chronos** and the attachment to time are chronology, chronic, and chronicle.[6]

(Or "chronometer.")

Chronos is a personification of Time; χρονος is the ordinary Greek word for time.[7]

[Here, I might have had more to say. I might have to say more. I have extra time (space).] In writing *Einstein on the Beach,* Robert Wilson and Philip Glass are said to have split up responsibility for the total time they wanted the work to occupy. "You take the first ten minutes, I'll take the next ten" — and so forth. [And here, I still need just a bit more.] In writing *Einstein on the Beach,* Robert Wilson and Philip ... well, Bob took ten, and Phil took...

---

5. from the entry "Chronos", in: *Wikipedia, the free encyclopedia,* http://en.wikipedia. org/wiki/Chronos accessed 10 March 2007.
6. Ibid.
7. Ibid.

4' 33"

In 1948, John Cage wrote a piano piece called *Dream*. It's notated using the alto clef — almost all in eighth-notes. There's a metronome marking and a one word instruction: *Rubato*. In nineteenth-century music, this word *rubato* is linked to "expression." And expression is linked to changing the flow of time ("taking time"): In the text of the *Prestissimo* second movement of Ludwig van Beethoven's Opus 109, after a phrase marked *un poco espressivo,* the composer writes *a tempo*. Does the word *rubato* disclose a fiction? — a fiction of the equivalence of the time in which we hear music and the time which may be signified by that music? In expressing presence or in being present, humans tell time variously and variably. Human performers cannot play beats of exactly equal length, for example. Perhaps this *rubato* discloses the disparity of musical time (flexible?) and measured time (systematized) — or between experience and description? The first time I played *Dream* in a public concert, Cage was there. I played the piece "from memory"; after the performance, someone asked a question: "What if the pianist gets lost?" Almost instantly Cage responded: "I think that would be *wonderful.*"[8] In the notation of some of Cage's piano works, there is an apparently unchanging proportional relationship between physical notational space and time. In the score for *TV Köln,* each complete system is defined as a representation of a constant (though unspecified) amount of time. Each system represents a duration equal to every other system — although the piece might last five minutes, or five years.

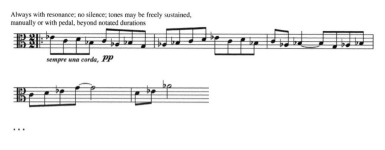

Always with resonance; no silence; tones may be freely sustained, manually or with pedal, beyond notated durations

*sempre una corda,* **PP**

...

8. At a birthday concert given for Cage by Boston Musica Viva on 4 November 1988 at the Longy School in Cambridge, Massachusetts.

*Time is Time: Temporal Signification in Music*

...

[9' 06"]

Always with resonance; no silence; tones may be freely sustained,
manually or with pedal, beyond notated durations

*sempre una corda,* **pp**

. . .

. . .

...

John Cage, *Dream*, 1948, excerpts.[9]

---

9. At the 2007 Orpheus Academy, Cage's *Dream* was performed as part of the presentation of this essay. *Dream* by John Cage © Copyright by Henmar Press, Inc. New York. Reproduced by kind permission of Peters Edition Limited, London.

13' 39"

In 1967, Marshall McLuhan's *The Medium is the Massage* was published. The title was misprinted—an "e" turned into an "a."[10] McLuhan seems to have intended "The Medium is the *Message.*" After the first copies arrived with the new wording—and is that "*Mass*-age," or "Mas-*sage*," or "Mass Age"?—McLuhan decided to adopt it. In this iconic text, we find:

Ours is a brand-new world of allatonceness. "Time" has ceased, "space" has vanished. We now live in a global village … a simultaneous happening… Electric circuitry profoundly involves men with one another. Information pours upon us, instantaneously and continuously. As soon as information is acquired, it is very rapidly replaced by still newer information. Our electrically-configured world has forced us to move from the habit of data classification to the mode of pattern recognition. We can no longer build serially, block-by-block, step-by-step, because instant communication insures that all factors of the environment and of experience co-exist in a state of active interplay.[11]

10. see http://www.marshallmcluhan.com accessed 21 August 2007.
11. Marshall McLuhan and Quentin Fiore, (coord.) Jerome Agel, *The Medium is the Massage,* New York 1967, p. 63.

In 1969, Kurt Vonnegut's novel *Slaughterhouse-five* appeared. In it, Vonnegut writes of Billy Pilgrim:

Listen:

Billy Pilgrim has come unstuck in time.

Billy has gone to sleep a senile widower and awakened on his wedding day. He has walked through a door in 1955 and come out another one in 1941. He has gone back through that door to find himself in 1963. He has seen his birth and death many times, he says, and pays random visits to all the events in between.

He says.

Billy is spastic in time, has no control over where he is going next, and the trips aren't necessarily fun. He is in a constant state of stage fright, he says, because he never knows what part of his life he is going to have to act in next.[12]

… And then, without any warning, Billy went to New York City, and got on an all-night radio program devoted to talk. He told about having come unstuck in time. He said, too, that he had been kidnapped by a flying saucer in 1967. The saucer was from the planet Tralfamadore, he said. He was taken to

---

12. Kurt Vonnegut, *Slaughterhouse-five; or, the children's crusade, a duty-dance with death*, New York 1969, p. 23.

Tralfamadore, where he was displayed naked in a zoo, he said. He was mated there with a former Earthling movie star named Montana Wildhack.[13]

He said.

Have all characters in novels come unstuck in time? Vonnegut is only acknowledging what is applicable to our reading of any text. We enter the text variously. It's polyvalent. We would not equate how much time we take in reading a group of words with the amount of time that such a "passage" in a book might signify. Why should we do that in music?

---

13. Ibid., p. 25.

18' 12"

Greenwich Mean Time (GMT) was established in 1675, when the Royal Observatory was built, as an aid to determine longitude at sea by mariners. The first time zone in the world was established by British railways on December 1, 1847 —[14]

(Incidentally, the same year as the first regular postage stamps were introduced in the U.S.)

—with GMT hand-carried on chronometers. About August 23, 1852, time signals were first transmitted by telegraph from the Royal Observatory, Greenwich. Even though 98% of Great Britain's public clocks were using GMT by 1855, it was not made Britain's legal time until August 2, 1880. Some old clocks from this period have two minute hands — one for the local time, one for GMT... [See Illustration 1.]

On November 2, 1868, New Zealand (then a British colony) officially adopted a standard time to be observed throughout the colony, and was perhaps the first country to do so. It was based on the longitude 172° 30' East of Greenwich, which is 11 hours 30 minutes ahead of GMT. This standard was known as New Zealand Mean Time.

Timekeeping on the American railroads in the mid nineteenth century was somewhat confused. Each railroad used its own standard time, usually based on the local time of its headquarters or most important terminus, and the railroad's train schedules were published using its own time. Some major railroad junctions served by several different railroads had a separate clock for each railroad, each showing a different time;

---

14. from the entry "Time zone", in: *Wikipedia, the free encyclopedia,* http://en.wikipedia. org/wiki/Time_zone accessed 12 March 2007.

the main station in Pittsburgh, Pennsylvania, for example, kept six different times. The confusion for travelers making a long journey involving several changes of train can be imagined.

Charles F. Dowd proposed a system of one-hour standard time zones for American railroads about 1863, although he published nothing on the matter at that time and did not consult railroad officials until 1869. In 1870, he proposed four ideal time zones (having north-south borders), the first centered on Washington, D.C., but by 1872 the first was centered 75°W of Greenwich, with geographic borders (for example, sections of the Appalachian Mountains). Dowd's system was never accepted by American railroads. Instead, U.S. and Canadian railroads implemented their own version on Sunday, November 18, 1883, also called "The Day of Two Noons", when each railroad station clock was reset as standard-time noon was reached within each time zone. The zones were named Intercolonial, Eastern, Central, Mountain, and Pacific. Within one year, 85% of all cities with populations over 10,000, about 200 cities, were using standard time. A notable exception was Detroit, Michigan (which is nearly half-way between the meridians of eastern time and central time, though actually a little closer to central), which kept local time until 1900, then tried Central Standard Time, local mean time, and Eastern Standard Time before a May 1915 ordinance settled on EST and was ratified by popular vote in August 1916. This hodgepodge ended when Standard zone times were formally adopted by the U.S. Congress on 19 March 1918 as the Standard Time Act...

Time zones based their time on Greenwich Mean Time (GMT, also called UT1), the mean solar time at longitude 0° (the Prime Meridian). But as a mean solar time, GMT is defined by the rotation of the Earth, which is not constant in rate. So, the rate of atomic clocks was annually changed or steered to closely match GMT. But on January 1, 1972 it became fixed, using predefined leap seconds instead of rate changes. This new time system is Coordinated Universal Time (UTC). Leap seconds are inserted to keep UTC within 0.9 seconds of UT1. In this way, local times continue to correspond approximately to mean solar time, while the effects of variations in Earth's rotation rate are confined to simple step changes that can be easily subtracted if a uniform time scale (International Atomic Time or TAI) is desired. With the implementation of UTC, nations began to use it in the definition of their time zones instead of GMT. As of 2005, most but not all nations have altered the definition of local time in this way (though many media outlets fail to make a distinction between GMT and UTC). Further change to the basis of time zones may occur if proposals to abandon leap seconds succeed.[15]

Since 1967, the International System of Units (SI) has defined the second as the period equal to 9,192,631,770 cycles of the radiation which corresponds to the transition between two energy levels of the ground state of the Cesium-133 atom.[16]

NIST-F1, the [United States'] primary time and frequency standard, is a cesium fountain atomic clock developed at the NIST laboratories in Boulder, Colorado. NIST-F1 contributes to the international group of atomic clocks that define Coordinated Universal Time (UTC), the official world time. Because NIST-F1 is among the most accurate clocks in the world, it makes UTC more accurate than ever before.

The uncertainty of NIST-F1 is continually...[17]

---

15. Ibid.
16. http://tf.nist.gov/timefreq/general/precision.htm accessed 28 March 2007.
17. http://tf.nist.gov/cesium/fountain.htm accessed 28 March 2007.

22' 45"

In *The Divine Comedy,* in Canto XVII in "Paradiso," Beatrice asks for a description of what the poet desires. In this text, Beatrice explains that such a description will help in the learning of how to say what is wanted. In Dante's "response," we read of "il punto a cui tutti li tempi son presenti" ("the point [the moment] in which all times are present").[18] Is this what T. S. Eliot signifies, in "The Dry Salvages"? He writes of:

> The point of intersection of the timeless
> With time...[19]

Frank Kermode considers "concord-fictions" in his *The Sense of an Ending.* A concord-fiction is a construct that may resemble, and allow us to help make sense of, our experience of life: I'd suggest *The Divine Comedy,* perhaps the Bible, Christo's *Wrapped Reichstag,* Cage's *4' 33".* Kermode writes:

> Men, like poets, rush 'into the middest,' *in medias res,* when they are born; they also die *in mediis rebus,* and to make sense of their span they need fictive concords with origins and ends, such as give meaning to lives and to poems.[20]

We're all in the middle.

---

18. Dante Alighieri, *La Commedia secondo l'antica vulgata a cura di Giorgio Petrocchi,* Milano 1967, XVII:17–18, at: http://world.std.com/~wij/dante/paradiso/par-17.html accessed 25 September 2007.
19. T. S. Eliot, "The Dry Salvages" (1941), *Four Quartets,* New York 1943, p. 27.
20. Frank Kermode, *The Sense of an Ending,* New York 1968, p. 7.

The End they imagine will reflect their irreductibly intermediary preoccupations. They fear it, and as far as we can see
have always done so; the End is a figure for their own deaths.
(So, perhaps, are all ends in fiction...)[21]

And in music.

What human need can be more profound than to humanize
the common death?[22]

And so here we are — *in medias res*. Kermode goes on to discuss
*aevum*:

> Aquinas ... had to invent this third order of duration, distinct
> from time and eternity. Needing to give it a name, he adopted
> a word he had heard Albert the Great use ... St. Thomas called
> this third order *aevum* ...
>
>   The formerly absolute distinction between time and eternity
> in Christian thought — between *nunc movens* with its begin-
> ning and end, and *nunc stans,* the perfect possession of endless
> life — acquired a third intermediate order based on this peculiar
> betwixt-and-between position of angels. But ... this concord-
> fiction soon proved that it had uses outside its immediate
> context, angelology. Because it served as a means of talking
> about certain aspects of human experience, it was humanized.
> It helped one to think about the sense men sometimes have of
> participating in some order of duration other than that of the

21. Ibid.
22. Ibid.

*nunc movens*— of being able, as it were, to do all that angels can. Such are those moments which Augustine calls the moments of the soul's attentiveness; less grandly, they are moments of what psychologists call 'temporal integration.' When Augustine recited his psalm he found in it a figure for the integration of past, present, and future which defies successive time... *Aevum* ... is a mode in which things can be perpetual without being eternal.

... It appeared quite soon that this *medium inter aeternitatem et tempus* had human uses. It contains beings (angels) with freedom of choice and immutable substance, in a creation which is in other respects determined. Although these beings are out of time, their acts have a before and an after. *Aevum,* you might say, is the time-order of novels.[23]

And music!

Characters in novels are independent of time and succession, but may and usually do seem to operate in time and succession; the *aevum* co-exists with temporal events at the moment of occurrence.[24]

And, I would propose: Events or ideas in musical compositions are independent of time and succession, but may and usually do seem to operate in time and succession; the *aevum* co-exists with

---

23. Ibid., p. 71–72.
24. Ibid., p. 72.

[27' 18"] temporal events at the moment of occurrence. Music —
and each piece of music — is a concord-fiction. In making music,
we make time audible, and we "explain" our experience of life.

In *Pour unnouveauroman,* Alain Robbe-Grillet has written:

> ... dans le récit moderne, on dirait que le temps se trouve
> coupé de sa temporalité. Il ne coule plus. Il n'accomplit plus
> rien.[25]
> [... in the modern narrative, one would say that time is cut off
> from its temporality. It no longer passes. It no longer accom-
> plishes anything.]

According to Kermode, in Robbe-Grillet's texts:

> The time of the novel is not related to any exterior norm of
> time. So, in *La Jalousie,* the narrator is explicitly 'unconcerned
> with chronology,' perceiving only that here and now in which
> memory, fantasy, anticipation of the future may intrude,
> though without sharp differentiation. The story does move
> forward, but without reference to 'real' time, or to the para-
> digms of real time familiar from conventional novels.[26]

In films, we have learned not to expect congruence. We know time
does not equal time — inside and outside a film. Although it's not
"suspension of disbelief," it is *aevum.* The rare films where a
lengthy event does occupy "real time" (*nunc movens*) are notable.
I'm thinking of the boiling potatoes in Chantal Akerman's *Jeanne
Dielman, 23 Quai du Commerce, 1080 Bruxelles.*[27] Compared to our
customary sense of filmic time, this is aberrant.

---

25. Alain Robbe-Grillet, *Pour unnouveauroman* (1963), Paris 1972, p. 168.
26. Kermode, p. 20.
27. *Jeanne Dielman, 23 Quai du Commerce, 1080 Bruxelles,* 201 minutes, Brussels and
Paris 1976.

In 1951, Cage visited the anechoic chamber at Harvard University. An anechoic chamber is a room designed in such a way that the walls, ceiling and floor absorb all sounds made in the room, rather than reflecting them as echoes.[28]

For certain engineering purposes, it is desirable to have as silent a situation as possible. Such a room is called an anechoic chamber, its six walls made of special material, a room without echoes. I entered one at Harvard University several years ago and heard two sounds, one high and one low. When I described them to the engineer in charge, he informed me that the high one was my nervous system in operation, the low one my blood in circulation. Until I die there will be sounds. And they will continue following my death. One need not fear about the future of music.[29]

There has been some skepticism about the reliability of the engineer's comments, especially being able to hear one's own nervous system (a mild case of tinnitus might be a more likely explanation for hearing a quiet, high-pitched sound). Whatever the truth of these explanations, Cage had gone to a place where he expected total silence, and yet heard sound.[30]

I have ... several new desires... first, to compose a piece of uninterrupted silence and sell it to Muzak Co. It will be 3 or $4^{1/2}$ minutes long—those being the standard lengths of "canned" music—and its title will be *Silent Prayer.* It will open with a single idea which I will attempt to make as seductive as the color and shape and fragrance of a flower. The ending will approach imperceptibly.[31]

---

28. from the entry "4' 33"," in: *Wikipedia, the free encyclopedia,* http://en.wikipedia.org/wiki/4'33 accessed 21 August 2006.
29. John Cage, "Experimental Music", *Silence,* Hanover, N.H. 1961, p. 8.
30. "4' 33"," *Wikipedia.*
31. John Cage, "A Composer's Confessions" (1948), in: *John Cage: Writer,* (ed.) Richard Kostelanetz, New York 1993, p. 43.

(The white paintings caught whatever fell on them; why did I not look at them with my magnifying glass? Only because I didn't yet have one? Do you agree with the statement: After all, nature is better than art?) Where does beauty begin and where does it end? Where it ends is where the artist begins.[32]

Actually what pushed me into it was not guts but the example of Robert Rauschenberg. His white paintings … when I saw those, I said, "Oh yes, I must. Otherwise I'm lagging, otherwise music is lagging."[33]

---

32. John Cage, "On Robert Rauschenberg, Artist, and His Work", *Silence*, p. 108.
33. John Cage, in: Richard Kostelanetz, *Conversing with Cage*, New York 1987, p. 71.

31' 51"

I

TACET

# II

TACET

# III

## TACET

John Cage, *4'33"*.[34]

---

34. At the 2007 Orpheus Academy, *4'33"* was performed as part of the presentation of this essay. *4'33"* by John Cage © Copyright by Henmar Press, Inc. New York. Reproduced by kind permission of Peters Edition Limited, London.

36' 24"

Wrote Isaac Newton:

Absolute, true, and mathematical time, in and of itself and of its own nature, without reference to anything external, flows uniformly and by another name is called duration. Relative, apparent, and common time is any sensible and external measure (precise or imprecise) of duration by means of motion; such a measure — for example, an hour, a day, a month, a year — is commonly used instead of true time.[35]

Schopenhauer:

Time is the condition of the *possibility* of succession, which could neither take place, nor be understood by us and expressed in words, without Time.[36]

And, then:

35. Isaac Newton, *The Principia: Mathematical Principles of Natural Philosophy* [*Principia,* 1726], (trans.) I. Bernard Cohen and Anne Whitman, Berkeley [3]1999, p. 408.
36. Arthur Schopenhauer, "On the Will in Nature", in: *On the Fourfold Root of the Principle of Sufficient Reason and On the Will in Nature: Two Essays,* (trans.) Mme. Karl Hillebrand, London [4]1907, p. 202.

Einstein showed that if time and space is measured using elec-
tromagnetic phenomena (like light bouncing between mir-
rors) then due to the constancy of the speed of light, time and
space become mathematically entangled together in a certain
way (called Minkowski time-space) which in turn results in
Lorentz transformation and in entanglement of all other
important derivative physical quantities (like energy, momentum, mass, force, etc.) in a certain 4-vectorial way...[37]

In the nineteenth century, in his *La Genese de l'idee du temps,* the
French philosopher Jean-Marie Guyau described time as a result
of human consciousness:

Time is not a condition, but rather a simple product of consciousness; time does not constitute consciousness, it derives
from it. Time is not an *a priori* form which we impose on phenomena; it is a set of relationships that experience establishes
among them. It is not a pre-established template that accepts
our perceptions and our feelings, but a river bed that they
erode and [at the same time] it is their spontaneous stream
through this bed.[38]

---

37. from the entry "Time", in: *Wikipedia, the free encyclopedia,* http://en.wikipedia.org/
wiki/Time accessed 28 March 2007.
38. Jean-Marie Guyau, in: *Guyau and the Idea of Time,* (trans.) John A. Michon,
Viviane Pouthas, Janet L. Jackson, Amsterdam and New York 1988, p. 145.

Guyau asks and answers a question:

Does our representation of time remain essentially discrete, or does it ultimately become continuous?... The mind, when representing time or any other dimension, in particular space, works predominantly in jumps, leaping over unseen intermediaries. There are fragments of time as well as of space, with clear interruptions and gaps. Only in the end, when impressions have been experienced repeatedly, do these gaps become smaller, finally reaching a vanishing point as a result of which a fusion between different intervals of perceived time can take place... Similarly, in space, we arrive at an uninterrupted, idealized view of things we do not actually see, as a result of some acquired momentum; and similarly also, we smoothly fill in the temporal gaps to ultimately conceive of time as a mathematical continuum.[39]

---

39. Ibid., pp. 143–44.

40' 57"

In his *The Illusion of the End* (published in 1988 as *L'illusion de la fin, ou, La Grève des événements*), Jean Baudrillard riffs on Canetti.[40]

One might suppose that the acceleration of modernity, or technology, events and media, of all exchanges — economic, political and sexual — has propelled us to 'escape velocity', with the result that we have flown free of the referential sphere of the real and of history. We are 'liberated' in every sense of the term, so liberated that we have taken leave of a certain space-time, passed beyond a certain horizon in which the real is possible because gravitation is still strong enough for things to be reflected and thus in some way to endure and have some consequence.[41]

Or, Baudrillard writes:

This time we have the opposite situation: history, meaning and progress are no longer able to reach their escape velocity. They are no longer able to pull away from this overdense body which slows their trajectory, which slows time to the point where, right now, the perception and imagination of the future are beyond us. All social, historical and temporal transcendence is absorbed by that mass in its silent immanence. Political events already lack sufficient energy of their own to

---

40. Wrote Elias Canetti: "A tormenting thought: as of a certain point, history was no longer *real*. Without noticing it, all mankind suddenly left reality; everything happening since then was supposedly not true." Elias Canetti, *The Human Province* [*Die Provinz des Menschen*, 1975], (trans.) Joachim Neugroschel, London 1985, p. 69.
41. Jean Baudrillard, *The Illusion of the End* [*L'illusion de la fin, ou, La Grève des événements*, 1988], (trans.) Chris Turner, Stanford, California 1994, p. 1.

move us: so they run on like a silent film for which we bear collective irresponsibility. History comes to an end here, not for want of actors, nor for want of violence (there will always be more violence), nor for want of events (there will always be more events, thanks be to the media and the news networks!), but by deceleration, indifference and stupefaction. It is no longer able to transcend itself, to envisage its own finality, to dream of its own end; it is being buried beneath its own immediate effect, worn out in special effects, imploding into current events.

Deep down, one cannot even speak of the end of history here, since history will not have time to catch up with its own end. Its effects are accelerating, but its meaning is slowing down inexorably. It will eventually come to a stop and be extinguished like light and time in vicinity of an infinitely dense mass.[42]

And then:

There is a third hypothesis, a third analogy. We are still speaking of a point of disappearance, a vanishing point, but this time in music. I shall call this the stereophonic effect. We are all obsessed with high fidelity, with the quality of musical 'reproduction'. At the consoles of our stereos, armed with our tuners, amplifiers and speakers, we mix, adjust settings, multiply tracks in pursuit of flawless sound. Is this still music? Where is the high fidelity threshold beyond which music disappears as such? It does not disappear for lack of music, but because it has passed this limit point; it disappears into the

---

42. Ibid., p. 2.

perfection of its materiality, into its own special effect. Beyond this point there is neither judgment nor aesthetic pleasure. It is the ecstasy of musicality, and its end... The disappearance of history is of the same order...

Right at the very heart of news, history threatens to disappear. At the heart of hi-fi, music threatens to disappear. At the heart of experimentation, the object of science threatens to disappear. At the heart of pornography, sexuality threatens to disappear. Everywhere we find the same stereophonic effect, the same absolute proximity to the real, the same effect of simulation.

By definition, this vanishing point, this point short...[43]

43. Ibid., pp. 5–6. At the 2007 Orpheus Academy, in response to a question about John Cage's place in the "construction of history" and how that might shape the understanding of temporality in his music, I said: "I think the paradigm for a musical 'work' that most of us have inherited encodes 'beginning, and middle, and end.' We might see Cage as opening the possibility for a music without end. Composers such as those with whom we are most familiar are makers, are givers of endings. If we were able to conceive — as I think Cage has — of a kind of music where there was not the necessity to finish the story, we would have a concord-fiction that would resemble our life a little bit more directly. Of course, our experiences of life are all different, and so it seems that a kind of art that would allow for that difference would be a good kind of art to have, in an egalitarian society. In a non-egalitarian society, there was nothing wrong with — and indeed there was something to be desired in — a hierarchical art where experience was mandated. Roland Barthes speaks of literature which is 'readerly' and 'writerly'. And he says that the old kind of art, that's the 'writerly' kind of art, is an art in which genius-creators, for example Beethoven, T. S. Eliot — these guys mandate an experience. And your only choice is what Barthes calls a 'referendum': you can either accept it or reject it. I think we see, in the twentieth-century, a few people — Thomas Pynchon, John Cage, maybe the minimalists — acknowledging that the role of the receiver can be more than passive. This allows art to be much more mutable, and much more useful." In the same question period, Ian Pace asked if one might see Cage's music as something like an object. Said I, "If Cage's music doesn't end, then it also doesn't begin. Cage suggests a kind of art that will not be art. It's in his description of Rauschenberg's paintings that I read to you: Where does beauty end? Where the artist begins. *4' 33"* negates 'creation' as we often understand it. One might imagine that the aim of Buddhist practice is simply to be. There is no start, no end. It's beginning, ending, 'presence' — allatonce. Time has collapsed."

45' 30"

In August 1959, Cage's "Lecture on Nothing" was published. It has a structure of whole-number rhythmic proportions, similar to structuring used in such music by Cage as the 1943 piano piece *A Room.* The printed text of the "Lecture on Nothing" is laid out in four columns that provide a proportional framework for reading:

Each line is to be read across the page from left to right, not down the columns in sequence. This should not be done in an artificial manner (which might result from an attempt to be too strictly faithful to the position of the words on the page), but with the *rubato* which one uses in everyday speech.[44]

```
I am here              ,        and there is nothing to say        .
                                                          If among you are
those who wish to get  somewhere            ,             let them leave at
any moment            .                        What we re–quire              is
silence               ;            but what silence requires
            is         that I go on talking
                                                    Give any one thought
            a push                  :        it falls down easily       .
;          but the pusher   and the pushed   *      pro–duce        that enter–
tainment        called        a dis–cussion               .
            Shall we have one later  ?
                              𝔴
Or            ,  we could simply de–cide                    not to have a dis–
cussion       .                   What ever you like .              But
now                       there are silences                       and the
words         make                help make                         the
silences       .
                                I have nothing to say
        and I am saying it                                    and that is
poetry                          as I need it              .
            This space of time                        is organized
    .                   We need not fear these        silences, —
                              𝔴
```

44. Cage, "Lecture on Nothing", *Silence,* London 1995, p. 109.

we may love them            .

                                                                This is a composed
talk                    ,              for I am making it
          just as I make            a piece of music.            It is like a glass
          of milk       .                      We need the       glass
and we need the        milk                   .      Or again    it is like an
empty glass                                into which                        at any
moment              anything                      may be poured
    .             As we go along          ,                      (who knows?)
               an i-dea may occur in this  talk                  .
                                        I have no idea            whether one will
               or not.                  If one does,             let it.          Re-
                                        ♍
gard it as something    seen                momentarily          ,                as
though              from a window        while traveling         .
If across Kansas        ,                   then, of course,     Kansas
    .             Arizona                           is more interesting,
almost too interesting    ,                 especially    for a New-Yorker    who is
being interested     in spite of himself    in everything.      Now he knows he
needs               the Kansas in him       .                   Kansas is like
nothing on earth        ,                   and for a New Yorker very refreshing.
It is like an empty glass ,                 nothing but wheat    ,                or
is it corn              ?                   Does it matter which ?
Kansas              has this about it:      at any instant,      one may leave it,
and whenever one wishes one may return to it    .
                                        ♍
Or you may leave it     forever         and never return to it   ,
          for we pos-sess nothing           .                   Our poetry now
          is the reali-zation               that we possess      nothing
    .             Anything                  therefore            is a delight
(since we do not    pos-sess it)            and thus             need not fear its loss
    .             We need not destroy the   past:               it is gone;
at any moment,      it might reappear and   seem to be           and be the present
    .             Would it be a             repetition?          Only if we thought we
owned it,          but since we don't,      it is free           and so are we

.
and how un–certain it is          Most anybody knows a–bout the future
                                  .

                                  ♏
What I am calling    poetry           is often called       content.
I myself           have called        it form               .          It is the continuity              of a piece of music.    Continuity        today,
when it is necessary    ,             is a demonstration                     of dis-
interestedness.    That is,           it is a proof         that our delight
lies in not        pos–sessing anything    .               Each moment
presents what happens  .                                   How different
this form sense is                from that        which is bound up with
memory:            themes          and secondary themes;    their struggle;
their development;    the climax;         the recapitulation    (which is the belief
that one may       own one's own home)   .                  But actually,
unlike the snail       ,          we carry our homes        within us,
                                  ♏
which enables us              to fly                        or to stay
, —                to enjoy           each.                 But beware of
that which is      breathtakingly        beautiful,         for at any moment
                   the telephone      may ring              or the airplane     .
come down in a     vacant lot           .                   A piece of string
or a sunset            ,                   possessing neither    ,
each acts                         and the continuity        happens
.                  Nothing more than     nothing            can be said.
Hearing            or making this     in music          is not different
—                  only simpler — 45

---

45. Ibid., pp. 109–11.

50' 03"

Time.gov is a website maintained by the United States govern-
ment with links to several agencies and organizations that keep
time. There's a lot of information at time.gov:

- **Atomic Time**, with the unit of duration the *Systeme
  International (SI)* second defined as the duration of
  9,192,631,770 cycles of radiation corresponding to the transition between two hyperfine levels of the ground state of
  cesium 133. **TAI** is the International **Atomic Time** scale, a statistical timescale based on a large number of **atomic** clocks.
- **Universal Time (UT)** is counted from 0 hours at midnight,
  with unit of duration the mean solar day, defined to be as uniform as possible despite variations in the rotation of the Earth.
  - **UT0** is the rotational **time** of a particular place of observa-
    tion. It is observed as the diurnal motion of stars or extrater-
    restrial radio sources.
  - **UT1** is computed by correcting UT0 for the effect of polar
    motion on the longitude of the observing site. It varies from
    uniformity because of the irregularities in the Earth's rotation.
- **Coordinated Universal Time (UTC)** differs from TAI by an
  integral number of seconds. UTC is kept within 0.9 seconds
  of UT1 by the introduction of one-second steps to UTC, the
  "**leap second.**" To date these steps have always been positive.
- **Dynamical Time** replaced *ephemeris time* as the independent
  argument in dynamical theories and ephemerides. Its unit of
  duration is based on the orbital motions of the Earth, Moon,
  and planets.
- **Terrestrial Time (TT)**, (or Terrestrial Dynamical **Time,**
  TDT), with unit of duration 86400 SI seconds on the geoid,
  is the independent argument of apparent *geocentric*
  ephemerides. TDT = TAI + 32.184 seconds.

- ○ **Barycentric Dynamical Time (TDB)**, is the independent argument of ephemerides and dynamical theories that are referred to the *solar system barycenter.* TDB varies from TT only by periodic variations.
- **Geocentric Coordinate Time (TCG)** is a *coordinate time* having its spatial origin at the center of mass of the Earth. TCG differs from TT as: TCG – TT = Lg x (JD – 2443144.5) x 86400 seconds, with Lg = 6.969291e-10.
- **Barycentric Coordinate Time (TCB)** is a *coordinate time* having its spatial origin at the solar system barycenter. TCB differs from TDB in rate. The two are related by: TCB – TDB = iLb x (JD – 2443144.5) x 86400 seconds, with Lb = 1.550505e-08.
- **Sidereal Time**, with unit of duration the period of the Earth's rotation with respect to a point nearly fixed with respect to the stars, is the hour angle of the vernal equinox.

**Delta T** is the **difference** between Earth rotational **time** (UT1) and dynamical **time** (TDT). Predicted values of **UT1 – UTC** are provided by the **Earth Orientation Department**...

**Julian Day Number** is a count of days elapsed since Greenwich mean noon on 1 January 4713 B.C., Julian proleptic calendar. The **Julian Date** is the Julian day number followed by the fraction of the day elapsed *since the preceding noon.*[46]

(So as it may be that faster travel, at least in part, led to the more regular keeping of time, and to the regularizing of time keeping,

---

46. from the entry "Systems of Time", http://tycho.usno.navy.mil/systime.html accessed 28 March 2007.

I'd suggest that the increasing range of keyboard instruments caused the need for increasingly equally-tempered tunings. It was only as the range of keyboard instruments expanded beyond the singable voice range that people began to be bothered — the Pythagorean comma so tangibly heard. Before the keyboard was that large, it didn't really matter. Before there were railroads, it didn't really matter that the time in Berlin was not the same as it was in Leipzig. If the railroads led to standard time zones, then the widening register of keyboard instruments eventually led to equal temperament!)

The Earth is constantly undergoing a deceleration caused by the braking action of the tides. Through the use of ancient observations of eclipses, it is possible to determine the average deceleration of the Earth to be roughly 1.4 milliseconds per day per century. This deceleration causes the Earth's rotational **time** to slow with respect to the **atomic** clock **time**. Thus, the definition of the ephemeris second embodied in Newcomb's motion of the Sun was implicitly equal to the average mean solar second over the eighteenth and nineteenth centuries. Modern studies have indicated that the epoch at which the mean solar day was exactly 86,400 SI seconds was approximately 1820. This is also the approximate mean epoch of the observations analyzed by Newcomb, ranging in date from 1750 to 1892, which resulted in the definition of the mean solar day on the scale of Ephemeris **Time**. Before then, the mean solar day was shorter than…[47]

---

47. from the entry "Leap Seconds", http://tycho.usno.navy.mil/leapsec.html accessed 28 March 2007. And so the solar day really was 86,400 seconds just at the time of the composition of Beethoven's Ninth Symphony! The introduction of Coordinated Universal Time (UTC), with its "leap-seconds", in 1972, coincides with such phasing-pieces as Steve Reich's *Six Pianos* (1973). (UTC and TAI are continually going out of phase with each other, only to be realigned by the introduction of leap seconds.)

[54' 36"]

PART THE SECOND
## Again minimalism again

In 1988, John Cage said:

> I can get my ears closer to it when something is being done than when
> something is being said even with words so much music goes up and
> down in a melodic way reaching a high point and a low point and com-
> ing to rest and in so doing seems to be saying something other music
> doesn't do that so much if it were saying something it seems to be say-
> ing it over and over to such an extent that you think that nothing's being
> said but something's being done because you can hear it being done and
> you can notice variations in it as it's being done...[48]

Isn't this a description of what is sometimes called "process"
music — minimalist music with a high degree of repetition, music
where the listener notices predominantly the *changes* in the material? No linear thinking, only "pattern recognition," Marshall
McLuhan might say.[49] And isn't Cage making a distinction
between this "something's-being-done" music, this process music,
and the teleological, narrative music we know in texts written by
traditional composers: Mozart, Beethoven — Beethoven with a
capital "B," or even "B –E–E–T," more on that later — or Johannes
Brahms, Elliott Carter, The Beatles, Milton Babbitt? In this
"something's-being-done" music, time passes. "Change" is represented.[50] The kind of rhythmically structured repetitive piece
where something is being done is already texted by Cage in his
piano piece *A Room* from 1943.

---

48. John Cage, *I-VI: MethodStructureIntentionDisciplineNotationIndeterminacyInter-
penetrationImitationDevotionCircumstancesVariableStructureNonunderstanding
ContingencyInconsistencyPerformance (Statistics for Industry and Technology)*, Cambridge,
Mass. 1990, pp. 306–308.
49. McLuhan and Fiore, p. 63.
50. In conventional opera, arias necessitate that the "action" stops, so that reflection
and comment can occur. This happens in concertos when cadenzas occur.

*Musical Example 1: John Cage, A Room, 1943, mm. 1–8.*

I like the title of Cage's piece *A Room* — a "room" is just what we might need, to gain awareness, consciousness, or presence in the moment. Cage says:

> One evening when I was still living at Grand Street and Monroe, Isamu Noguchi came to visit me. There was nothing in the room (no furniture, no paintings). The floor was covered wall to wall, with cocoa matting. The windows had no curtains, no drapes. Isamu Noguchi said, "An old shoe would look beautiful in this room."[51]

So, the perfect emptiness. Beauty ends, where the artist begins, Cage says.[52] Art is a context, or a frame, or a mode of being.

Paul Hindemith tells us that the emotions, the feelings we have when we listen to music are not the same as "real" feelings we experience as a result of life experiences. Hindemith says this is clear because the progression from one intense feeling to another is sometimes accomplished very quickly in music (and we are not — most of us — "insane").[53] Hearing music does require time.

---

51. John Cage, "How to Pass, Kick, Fall and Run," *A Year From Monday: New Lectures and Writings,* Middletown, Connecticut 1967, p. 133.
52. Cage, *Silence,* p. 108.
53. "Real feelings need a certain interval of time to develop, reach their climax, and fade again; reactions to music, however, may change as fast as musical phrases do; they may spring up in full intensity at any given moment and disappear entirely when the musical pattern that provoked them ends or changes. Thus these reactions may, within a few instants, skip from the most profound grief to utter hilarity and on to complacency, without causing any discomfort to the mind experiencing them, as would be the case with a rapid succession of real feelings. In fact, if it happened with real feelings, we could be sure that it could be only in the event of slight insanity." Paul Hindemith, "Emotion in Music", *A Composer's World, Horizons, and Limitations,* Cambridge, Mass. 1952, p. 38. See also Stephen Davies, "The Expression of Emotion in Music", *Themes in the Philosophy of Music,* Oxford and New York 2003, pp. 134–51, and Stephen Davies, *Musical Meaning: and Expression,* Ithaca, N.Y. and London 1994.

Is the clock-measured time that passes while listening necessarily equal to "time" music might signify? We don't make such an assumption in reading a novel, or in watching a film. (I've already mentioned the rare case of a film like Chantal Akerman's *Jeanne Dielman* where some lengthy events do unfold in "real time.")[54] It's only a rare piece of visual art, even clearly representational visual art, in which the physical dimensions of the work equal the space represented. In landscapes, the signified space is often much greater. At the other extreme, there are conspicuously oversized representations — the lead books of Anselm Kiefer's census,[55] Claes Oldenburg's clothespin, Rodin's figure of Balzac. Visual art allows us to experience space variously. Why limit music to unbendingly rigid temporal signification? Might it be that the rapid change of Hindemith's feelings may be accounted for — not because these emotional responses are not "real," but — because the agency of music allows us to travel through, or experience time variously?

Of course, it seems to be true that schizophrenic patients cannot distinguish the difference between past, present, and future — or that the distinguishing seems pointless. If past, present, and future experience "present" (pre · sent) a high level of sameness, then no distinction may be possible. Very repetitive music can so alter our sense of reality/time. Jonathan Kramer recounts an experience:[56]

> I attended about three hours of an 18-hour performance of Erik Satie's *Pages mystiques* (1893) the middle movement of which is the infamous *Vexations*. This movement consists of four eight-bar phrases (the bar-lines are not notated) ... Satie indicates that the movement is to be

---

54. A participant in the Orpheus Academy pointed out to me that there's another entire category of films where actions are sometimes represented in "real time" — porn!

55. Anselm Kiefer, *Volkszählung* (1991), Hamburger Bahnhof, Berlin.

56. A large portion of this essay grew from a presentation I made at Columbia University at the invitation of Jonathan Kramer (and Tristan Murail). The happy specter of Kramer hung over the 2007 Orpheus Academy. In papers and question periods, his ideas appeared many times. Perhaps this itself challenges our customary sense of "time" — posthumously Jonathan was at this Academy about it.

played 840 times in succession. Although this instruction may have been one of the composer's cryptic witticisms ... several present-day musicians have decided to take it quite seriously and literally. Thus a team of pianists agreed to play *Vexations* at the Oberlin Conservatory, in 1971. Every twenty minutes a new pianist took over, as unobtrusively as possible. The performers tried to play evenly and to imitate each other tonally, so that every repetition was close to being the same.

... When I first entered the concert, I listened linearly. But I soon exhausted the information content of the work. It became totally redundant. For a brief period I felt myself getting bored, becoming imprisoned by a hopelessly repetitive piece. Time was getting slower and slower, threatening to stop.

But then I found myself moving into a different listening mode. I was entering the vertical time of the piece. My present expanded, as I forgot about the music's past and future. I was no longer bored. And I was no longer frustrated, because I had given up expecting. I had left behind my habits of teleological listening. I found myself fascinated with what I was hearing. The music was not simply a context for meditation, introspection, or daydreaming. I was *listening*... I became incredibly sensitive to even the smallest performance nuance, to an extent impossible when confronting the high information content of traditional music.

After what seemed like forty minutes I left. My watch told me that I had listened for three hours.[57]

So, a considerable disparity of times — inside and outside the music, inside and outside the mind.

La Monte Young speculated that certain patterns of repetitive music could induce specific brain response in listeners[58] — Alpha waves perhaps? Hearing parts of Young's piece *The Well-Tuned Piano* might be akin to taking mind-altering drugs. Perhaps the titles of some sections of *The Well-Tuned Piano* bear that out: *The Homage to Brahms Variation* of *The Theme of The Dawn of Eternal*

---

57. Jonathan Kramer, *The Time of Music: new meanings, new temporalities, new listening strategies,* New York 1988, pp. 378–79.
58. See, for example, La Monte Young, "Notes on *The Well-Tuned Piano*", from the notes accompanying the recording *The Well-Tuned Piano 81 X 25,* New York 1987, p. 6.

*Time* in *The Deepest Pool,* for example! I believe it's fair to say that La Monte Young holds tempered tuning to be a social ill. *The Well-Tuned Piano* was realized on a specially tuned Bösendorfer Imperial concert grand. (The tuning may take several weeks to achieve.) The resulting intervals are unlike anything on the stand-ard modern piano, with its flattened, tempered intervals. Young might say that by constantly listening to tempered scales, we are missing out on music's potential to most powerfully or positively affect our mental chemistry. The entire *Well-Tuned Piano* is four, five, or even six hours long. (I wonder about the recent number of six-hour long piano pieces: Michael Finnissy's *The History of Photography in Sound,* Alvin Curran's *Inner Cities,* Frederic Rzewski's even longer *The Road.* Are there more? When will we have the first twenty-four-long piano piece?) [59]

Although commentators have sometimes explained Minimalist music as reaction to the high complexity of mid-twentieth century art music, it might be seen as a far greater change—a change in musical time keeping, or signification. Gone is the paradigm of narration. Gone is the steady model of beginning, middle, and end. We occupy the middle with minimalism. And in music this probably has a lot to do with the declining (or at least reclining!) authority of the composer, of the composer as genius/creator, of the composer as "god"—supplying beginnings and endings. We are *in medias res,* and minimalist music acknowledges it. Of course, this change takes in much more than music: consider Roland Barthes' death of the author,[60] McLuhan's description of the "allatonceness" of life in our world.[61] Here, perhaps, we are contemplating the end of God, the death of God, in our society?[62]

---

59. I imagine a twenty-four-hour-long performance given by a team of pianists, sometimes playing simultaneously and overlapping a large number of pieces from the canonic piano repertory. I plan to call the performance, *Piano Music.*
60. Roland Barthes, "The Death of the Author", *Image— Music— Text,* (trans.) Stephen Heath, New York 1977, pp. 142–48.
61. Op. cit.
62. Barthes' pronouncement of authorial death was made in 1967, McLuhan's "alla-tonceness" was described in 1967. Vatican II, which began the transition to the use of vernacular languages in the celebration of the Mass, concluded in 1965. *Time* Magazine's much discussed cover posing the question "Is God Dead?" appeared on the issue of 8 April 1966.

Differing temporal relationships, significations, and uses of time can be discerned in several examples of American minimalist music. Consider Philip Glass's *Mad Rush,* a keyboard piece from about 1980, although written down, in the form it's published, around 1988. The piece features a lot of repetition. There are many-times recurring phrases using simple tonal harmony. The music might seem to use some language of pop music — producing some almost familiar *vin ordinaire.* There are recurring contrasting loud sections with quick surface activity. The underlying progression remains the same in the active music and in the quiet music; the rate of harmonic change is fairly constant throughout sixteen minutes or so.

*Musical Example 2: Philip Glass, Mad Rush, mm. 3–6.*

Even though not very much changes during *Mad Rush,* the subtly recentered experience of the hearer may offer a sort of "development," as repeated material is encountered anew. This sense comes from the hearer — more than from the text.[63] I'm hesitating to say "exactly repeated" material, remembering how Kramer describes our heightened awareness of performance variations in repeated

---

63. "Repetition is a form of change," said Brian Eno. See Alex Ross, *The Rest is Noise: Listening to the Twentieth Century,* New York 2007, p. 511.

text. Just as we learn the language of tonal harmony, we learn past, present, and future. We learn it from our verbal languages, from our religions. This model pervades Western culture and affects the reception of music. It affects my reception of *Mad Rush*. Some psychologists imagine that animals don't share this past/present/future. Even other humans may not share it (or might conceive it differently), if untouched by cultural artifacts or constructs that pervasively encode a Western sense of "beginning, middle, and end."[64]

When Philip Glass lived in Paris, the immediate provocation for his new style (his minimalist "practice") was his work transcribing music of Ravi Shankar. It's a complicated cross-pollination. Shankar's particular presentation of Karnatic music was itself aimed at Western ears and sensibilities.[65] Yet, some sense of being in the moment, of the cycles of life, may be borrowed and encoded in Glass's minimalism. And there is an element of exoticism in minimalism; we could see it as an exoticism practice. (Perhaps everything tasty in European culture was taken, pilfered, or stolen from the East — and then the Americas. The seasoning of food with pepper in the Middle Ages? "Turkish" music in Mozart's Vienna? The wonderful chocolate we eat in Belgium or Holland? Or Pepys drinking his? Tomatoes, Chopin writing mazurkas in Paris, Ravi Shankar with The Beatles in London, Debussy's "gamelan" sounds?) Glass has acknowledged his debt — especially to the South Indian Kathakali theater, in which the stories told are both communal and cyclic. It is a non-authoritarian art. And Glass has discussed his experience of working on a production of *Play* by Samuel Beckett: the audience, Glass says, is

---

64. Guyau speculates about animals and time. Then there's the strong linguistic determinism of Benjamin Lee Whorf. More recent studies by Lera Broditsky have considered conceptual differences in thinking about time on the part of speakers of English and Mandarin. See Lera Broditsky, "Does language shape thought?: Mandarin and English Speakers' Conceptions of time", *Cognitive Psychology*, 43:1 (August 2001), pp. 1–22.

65. See the celebrated recording *Sounds of India* (1968), New York 1989, in which Shankar includes short spoken and played lessons along with the music he performs. Modification is inherent to exoticism practices: in some Chinese restaurants in New York City, along with the regular menu, there is also a "Chinese" menu. Less-modified dishes are listed there — the duck-tongue dishes, for example.

necessary to complete the work, differently each night for each person.[66] Cultural paradigms are inextricable from the reception of art, and from the experience of life I suppose. Cage writes:

> When I first began to study Oriental philosophy, I also wondered about whether it was mine to study... At Darmstadt I was talking about the reason back of pulverization and fragmentation ... I said, "We take things apart in order that they may become the Buddha. And if that seems too Oriental an idea for you," I said, "Remember the early Christian Gnostic statement, "Split the stick and there is Jesus!"[67]

Susan McClary has observed that the kind of two-against-three passage that begins *Mad Rush* recalls piano music by Robert Schumann or Johannes Brahms. McClary writes of "subjective interiority" or at least the simulation of it by Glass. (She's describing another similar piece by Glass called *Opening*.)[68] So this part of the music could be a nineteenth-century, middle-of-the-keyboard, character piece — except for all the repetition, of course. This might be seen as an "appropriation." Not a literal appropriation, but a stylistic, textural approximation of something familiar, something old. Just one of many other examples is a work called *Endangered Species* by Alvin Curran. (I'm referring to the piano solo; there's another of Curran's pieces that has this name too.) Curran wrote *Endangered Species* on oblong music paper: an early nineteenth-century signification. It's in E Major, more or less, and marked "Mit innigste Empfindung": an allusion to Beethoven's E-Major Piano Sonata, Opus 109. Curran's piece tropes Schumann's *Arabeske*. Curran inscribed an early version of *Endangered Species*, "To Susan, from Eusebius," and identified himself by signing the name of the piece's composer as an anagram of his name: Carl van Ruin!

---

66. Philip Glass, *Music by Philip Glass,* (ed.) Robert J. Jones, New York 1987, pp. 35–37.
67. John Cage, "How to Kick, Fall, and Run", p. 136.
68. Susan McClary, "Reveling in the Ruble: The Postmodern Condition", *Conventional Wisdom: The Content of Musical Form,* Berkeley and Los Angeles 2000, p. 142.

*Musical Example 3: Alvin Curran, Endangered Species, mm. 1–4.*

Some might want to align the spare, even austere simplicity of Glass's music, especially early pieces like *Two Pages,* or even *Music in Twelve Parts,* with the high architectural modernism of Mies van der Rohe. "Less is more," Mies famously repeated.[69] Of course, by the 1960s, American architects like Robert Venturi were well into post-modernism, with lots of appropriation: the Palladian façade of the house Venturi built for his mother (1961–64). Or, a bit later, the huge pediment that tops Philip Johnson's 1984 A.T. & T. Building (now the Sony Building) in New York City — a pediment reminiscent of what one could see, in vastly smaller scale, at the top of a piece of furniture, a chest by Chippendale. No "form follows function" here. In answer to modernism's "Less is more," Robert Venturi wrote, in 1966, "Less is a bore," and also, "More is not less."[70] Artists like Roy Lichtenstein, or David Salle appropriated or borrowed image surfaces, juxtaposing them, blowing them up, changing dimensions, changing scale. Glass's or Curran's harkenings to, or resizing of simple nineteenth-century domestic piano music are appropriatively (and appropriately) "postmodern."[71]

How is "time" a part of our sense of artistic modernity? Friedrich Schelling opined: "Architektur ist überhaupt die erstarrte Musik."

---

69. The phrase appears already in Robert Browning's poem "Andrea del Sarto", first published in 1855. See *Robert Browning: The Major Works,* (ed.) Adam Roberts, Oxford 2005, p. 241.
70. Robert Venturi, *Complexity and Contradiction in Architecture,* New York 1966, p. 17 and p. 16.
71. John Butt compares a considerable number of differing views of what constitutes "Modern" and "Postmodern." See John Butt, *Playing with History: The Historical Approach to Musical Performance,* Cambridge 2002, pp. 125–64.

("Overall architecture is frozen music.")[72] Goethe suggested modifying this description of architecture, using the words: "vers-
tummte Tonkunst"[73] ("silenced musical composition"). Is the cool
symmetry of the Seagram's Building "erstarrte Musik", a stoppage
of time, an aria? Is the complex, polysurfaced painting *F111* by
James Rosenquist, an encoding, a visualization, of change through
time — of the movement from past to future through the narrow
slit of now? If there is, in traditional composed music, a tension
between *aevum* inside and the time (*nunc movens*) outside the
work, then it is this friction which is the material of minimalist
music. The friction is brought inside the piece. (Traveling in our
cars, we are aware of our relatively slow approach to what we see
ahead while being aware at the same time of the seemingly more
rapid motion glimpsed through the side windows.) Perhaps bringing this friction inside the piece is itself a transitional phase of
development. If Modernism might be seen to begin with the
Enlightenment, or, in music, with the rise of the "composer" and
the composer's ego in the late eighteenth and early nineteenth centuries, then minimalism may be some final mannerist phase, a
composing out, of the Modern.

To me, with my particular learned sensibility, there are passages in
Franz Schubert's piano sonatas that almost seem to turn into minimalist loops. Charles Rosen describes the alternation of five-bar
phrases centered on the pitches C, and B, and C, and B again, in
the development of the first movement of Schubert's A-Major
Sonata, D. 959, as a sort of harmonic "stasis."[74] I might mention
some measures from the slow movement of the D-Major Sonata,
D. 850.[75] But these are foreshadowings. I've been asked whether
*Bolero* is minimalist music. (Probably not.) I might mention that

---

72. Friedrich Wilhelm Joseph von Schelling, *The Philosophy of Art* [*Die Philosophie der Kunst*, 1809], (trans.) Douglas W. Stott, Minneapolis 1989, p. 177. Perhaps "fixed" is a better translation of "erstarrte."
73. Goethe, *Maximen und Reflexionen*, in: *Werke* (Hamburger Ausgabe), 12 (1953), p. 474.
74. Beginning in m. 130. See Charles Rosen, *Sonata Forms*, New York 1988, pp. 360–62.
75. mm. 178–180.

as a kid Glass listened more to Schubert's music than to Beethoven's — conditioning for later? Glass's father owned a store, and Glass has recounted somewhat humorously that his father brought home the stuff that didn't sell, recordings of Schubert's sonatas, for example.[76] Was listening to these unsold recordings a casual, coincidental resistance to market forces? Was this, or did it cause some inverse or contrarian inclination against the then normative, commercial classical music business?

Glass's or Curran's appropriation of nineteenth-century, middle-of-the-keyboard piano gestures is a kind of unfastening from time.[77] Of course, such appropriation in the late twentieth century is a dissociation of gesture or language from its initial chronological identity; but, it is also an unfastening, of the expectations of temporal progress, or expectations of change, that operate in music like Schumann's or Beethoven's. This minimalism is the expansion of, or dwelling, or focusing on something that might have passed in a moment. It's a scrutiny of detail. It's troping. *Leoninus in Perotinus?* Brahms reading Beethoven? Glass doing Schumann!

Troping can be seen as remodeling, sometimes a building within, or a new annexing to something that remains; time has passed since the making of the primary edifice. Some post-production artists today have discovered previously unimagined spaces within, scrutinizing art icons, troping through technology. Leif Inge has made *9 Beet Stretch* by stretching out a recording of Beethoven's Ninth Symphony — there's the "B-E-E-T" — so that the music lasts twenty-four hours. Every thing happens at real pitch, and events like the entry of the many players in a violin section on a strong note, are revealed to contain previously unheard complexity.[78] Surface activity over slow underlying motion:

---

76. See, for example, text from a website pertaining to Glass's and Robert Wilson's *Monsters of Grace* cited in: Wheeler Winston Dixon, *The Second Century of Cinema: The Past and Future of the Moving Image*, Albany, N.Y. 2000, p. 216.

77. I was reluctant to use "unstuck" again. Almost as I spoke Kurt Vonnegut's word during my first presentation on the first day of the 2007 Orpheus Academy, 11 April 2007, Vonnegut died.

78. See Leif Inge, *9 Beet Stretch*, http://www.notamo2.no/9/ accessed 29 October 2007.

Beethoven becomes Minimalism. Similarly, Douglas Gordon has made *Twenty-four Psycho,* a silent, daylong stretch-out of Alfred Hitchcock's film *Psycho.* Films are made up of discrete frames, of course, and each *Psycho* frame occupies the screen for about a second in Gordon's reading. Is this "giving up expecting," or is it only expecting?

Although Glass's music generally repeats a simple pattern of harmonic change many times over, other kinds of minimalist music extend a single pitch or a single, unchanging harmonic area, possibly with timbral shifts, or surface rhythmic activity. Perhaps these distinct minimalisms offer a difference between "repeating" a short event and actually "stopping" time? Perhaps this extended-harmonic-area minimalism juxtaposes the external passage of time with the signification of stopped-time in the music?[79] Extreme examples might come from such California composers as James Tenney, or Harold Budd. A piano piece by the honorary Californian Alvin Curran, *Hope Street Tunnel Blues III,* extends a bent A-flat major-minor chord for about ten minutes. Eventually the harmony changes. When the change occurs it's an event of strong impact. The physical action of the piece is significant. *Hope Street Tunnel Blues III* might be allied to the late twentieth-century phenomenon of "extreme sports"—for the performer, playing this fast, repetitve music may cause considerable physical pain. It's like running a marathon. Perhaps these physical motions are as much the music as the sounds themselves? It's a ritual. And a struggle that is a ritual. The intense awareness of an ongoing physical task comprised of many quick gestures in time, is juxtaposed with musical material that for long periods seems not to move.

(By the way, does Curran's piece intertextualize Paul Simon's "Graceland"—or "Frankie and Johnny"?) I've wondered if this music is a sort of "position paper" by Curran (influenced by Cornelius Cardew)—never to be performed?

---

79. "Stop time" describes a feature of early ragtime. In jazz or rap, there's the "break" which resembles the time stoppage of the opera aria.

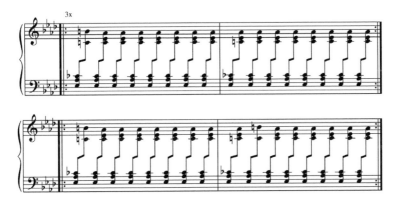

*Musical Example 4: Alvin Curran, Hope Street Tunnel Blues III, mm. 11–14.*

Robert Fink has described how Minimal music may mirror life in the consumer society of today. In the introduction of his book *Repeating Ourselves,* he considers several people on a late Friday night:

> In a converted warehouse near the urban core, hundreds of dancers are moving in rhythm to highly repetitive electronic music; many of them are under the influence of controlled substances…
>
> A solitary late-night shopper wheels her cart down the soup aisle of a nearby supermarket; she finds the repeating pattern of the colored labels vaguely relaxing as she glides by. (Clinical monitoring of her eye-blink rate would show that she has entered the first stage of hypnoid trance…
>
> A writer sits in his suburban study watching a videotape of network television. He has almost 100 sets of tapes, 24 hours of every channel available from his local cable provider on a given day… He is watching them all, trying to make sense of the torrential flow of information… Downtown, a junior advertising executive sits in a conference room with a computer printout. He is engaged in a strangely similar task, tallying against the agency's media plan the thousands of television and radio buys they executed last week for a major soft-drink account…
>
> A college student sets out to read 150 pages of an overdue sociology assignment… She picks out her favorite relaxing-and-study music, a bargain reissue … of Vivaldi violin concertos that includes the famous *Four Seasons.* She figures that if she mixes up the 20-odd movements on

the 65-minute CD with random and repeat play, she should have enough familiar music in the background...

... The girl's mother silently enters the darkened bedroom of her six-year-old son. The headphones have slipped off, so she gently puts them back before flipping the cassette tape over. The music begins again ... and she thinks, not for the first time, how strange it is that the Suzuki teacher demands they listen to the same few tracks over and over, even when sleeping...

... A sophomore composition major is fiddling with a keyboard and computer sequencing software. She has been listening obsessively to Steve Reich's 1976 *Music for Eighteen Musicians* and, trying to get the same effect, has created several slow, overlapping analog-string melodies and some faster figures for a sampled marimba... She will never show this to her composition teacher... To tell the truth, if he asked her why anybody should care about two idiotic minimal loops repeating over and over and slowly going out of phase, she'd have no answer.

Except that it sounds like, *feels* like...

Her life.[80]

And is that Eliot's:

The point of intersection of the timeless
With time...[81]

Is that Baudrillard's "result":

... that we have flown free of the referential sphere of the real and of history. We are 'liberated' in every sense of the term, so liberated that we have taken leave of a certain space-time...[82]

---

It may be that the nature of the piano's resonance gives it an inher-

---

80. Robert Fink, *Repeating Ourselves: American Minimal Music as Cultural Practice*, Berkeley, California 2006, pp. 1–3.
81. Op. cit.
82. Op. cit.

ently backward-looking nature. The piano, and especially the modern piano, is a great big decrescendo machine. Almost as soon as a sound is produced it's fading, dying. So it's not an accident that the piano is generally, at least on the stage, colored black. It's a coffin. It's an instrument of death. The death of each sound, at least. And perhaps piano music is prone to be summarizing, wrapping up? It's also prone to showing ways to the future.[83] "Ma fin est mon commencement..."[84] T. S. Eliot writes:

> And to make an end is to make a beginning.
> The end is where we start from...[85]

In William Duckworth's piano pieces *The Time Curve Preludes* (1977–1978), there may be some signification of the time-space continuity that physicists model. In this music, time may "slow down," space may contract. Kyle Gann has called Duckworth's pieces the first musical "post-minimalism."[86] Against a general practice of repetition, other style practices intrude. The power of the piano to allow us to hear the immediate past, is underlined by the use, in the piece, of metal weights on some of the piano's bass keys. These weights hold down low notes, specified for each of the twenty-four preludes, making drones as the music is played. With only small possibilities for modifying the sound of a note after it has begun, pianists, in initially striking a note, are determining the nature of the note's continuation and decay. As we listen to a long note on the piano, we are hearing the results of actions already made. (Piano playing does offer the possibility of recontextualizing sounds. How the "next note" is played can strongly affect our "hearing" of what we have already taken in.) The necessity to move the weights before each of Duckworth's preludes

---

83. I explored this notion in a concert project called *Piano Future!* at New England Conservatory in Boston in January 2007. See http://concerts.newenglandconservatory.edu/index.php?Date_Year=2007&Date_Month=01&Date_Day=23 accessed 29 October 2007.
84. Text from Machaut's eponymous three-voiced rondeau.
85. T. S. Eliot, "Little Gidding" (1942), *Four Quartets,* New York 1943, p. 38.
86. See Kyle Gann, "A Forrest from the Seeds of Minimalism: An Essay on Postminimal and Totalist Music", http://www.kylegann.com/postminimalism.html accessed 8 December 2007.

yields a measured ritual of silent gestures that might suggest a priest moving vessels at the altar in preparing to celebrate communion.

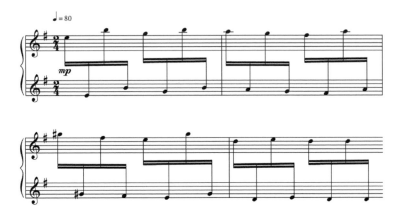

*Musical Example 5: William Duckworth, The Time Curve Preludes, Book 1, No. 11, mm. 1–4.*

The eleventh of Duckworth's preludes does seem to hark to some "tradition" of religious music — the chant of a forgotten monastic order? So it looks back in at least two ways — to a past that never was (as Richard Taruskin says of neo-classicism)[87] and especially, at cadence points, to the immediate past. We hear the lingering residue of the drones, of sound dissipating in time.[88]

---

87. Richard Taruskin, "Back to Whom? Neoclassicism as Ideology", *19th-Century Music* 16, no. 3 (Spring 1993), pp. 286–302.

88. Ian Pace asked me whether there was a fascist bent to the notion of aesthetic "purity" in this prelude, akin to what he discerns in Carl Orff's *Carmina Burana*. It's a difficult judgment to make. Our sense of what is appropriate in borrowing, allusion, or suggestion is temporary: Gershwin's "chinoserie" in the "I Got Rhythm" Variations? Mickey Rooney's Japanese caricature in *Breakfast at Tiffany's*? Meredith Monk's *Dolmen Music*? Chopin's Mazurkas?

89. See Theodor Adorno, "Stravinsky: A Dialectical Portrait" (1962), in: *Quasi Una Fantasia: Essays on Modern Music*, (trans.) Rodney Livingstone, London 1998, pp. 145–77, and Theodor Adorno, *Philosophy of Modern Music* [*Philosophie der neuen Musik*, 1948], (trans.) Anne G. Mitchell and Wesley V. Blomster, New York and London 2003, also Milan Kundera's detailed rebuttal of Adorno's position, Milan Kundera, "Improvisation in Homage to Stravinsky", in: *Testaments Betrayed: A Essay in Nine Parts*, (trans.) Linda Asher, New York 1995, pp. 53–95.

Theodor Adorno maintained that music with highly repetitive rhythm resembled (was?) fascism. He was criticizing Stravinsky.[89] Perhaps only change, only development — linear development — can signify humanity. Why did Olivier Messiaen (another possible progenitor of minimalism in music) take up what he termed "non-retrogradable" rhythms? — rhythm palindromes that literally hold their identity forward or backward? Well, there's less possibility for change. There's less possibility for direction. In Messiaen's harmony, increasing inclusion of traditionally "dominant" elements in resolutions undermines direction. Past is present is future. Increasingly, "all times are present" ("tutti li tempi son presenti"). Although Adorno might have held art to be an expression of humanity, or categorized art as expression, a great deal of modernist literature has sought to take the writer's voice, or intention itself, out of text. Artists have tried "automatic writing," "stream of consciousness," drip painting. Today video games provide multiple pathways and multiple endings for their players; they are hypertexts of play. How can a pre-written text mimic or signify life experience where the future actually *is* unknown? The making of an art that would not be "expressive" — is this what Cage suggests when he says, "I have nothing to say and I am saying it"?[90] Or what Jacques Derrida signified in saying, "Pardon de ne vouloir dire."[91] He was talking about Abraham's "predicament" (what a word!). Derrida was talking about the nature of "secrets" in fixed literary texts. We the readers are often "in" on the secret. We know what God said to Abraham, just as we know what's going to happen to, what's scripted for, what awaits the sonata movement's second theme. Can this be real action? Or is it Chekhov's gun, glimpsed in the first act of a play, and inevitably going off later?[92] So how can

---

90. Cage, "Lecture on Nothing", p. 109.
91. Jacques Derrida, from a paper given at New York University, see "Literature in Secret: An Impossible Filiation", (trans.) Adam Kotsko, http://www.adamkotsko.com/weblog/Derrida.Literature.In.Secret.pdf accessed 19 September 2007.
92. See, for example, Donald Rayfield, Anton Chekhov: *A Life*, New York 1997. Perhaps this "gun" first belonged to V. I. Nemirovich-Danchenko, see Cynthia Carlile, Sharon McKee, Andrei Mikhailovich Turkov, *Anton Chekhov and His Times*, Fayetteville, Arkansas 1995, p. 75.

time pass if there's a text? If we want to enter the realm of "real" experience, the actual transport from now to a future moment — must we have an art with uncertainty, with actual chance in it?

A clichéd gesture of later twentieth-century pop music is the "fade-out." If there's no possibility of satisfying conclusions — where's the future-affirming, third-on-the-top cadence of Beethoven's Fourth Piano Concerto? — if cadences lack sincerity, then what possibilities are there for an ending? It doesn't, anymore, convince to write, read, or utter, "The End." With the fade-out, technology offered the electronic equivalent of the band walking over the hill, off into the distance, *lontano*. In the absence of a convincing wrap-up or finale, one can only stop!

# NOTATION, TIME AND THE PERFORMER'S RELATIONSHIP TO THE SCORE IN CONTEMPORARY MUSIC

*Ian Pace*

*To Mark Knoop*

## I.
## THE PERFORMER'S READING OF GRAND NARRATIVES

There is a certain narrative construction of Western musical history, concerning development of the composer-performer relationship and the concomitant evolution of musical notation,
which is familiar and at least tacitly accepted by many. This narrative goes roughly as follows: in the Middle Ages and to a lesser
extent to the Renaissance, musical scores provided only a bare out-
line of the music, with much to be filled in by the performer or
performers, who freely improvising within conventions which
were for the most part communicated verbally and were highly
specific to region or locality. By the Baroque Era, composers had
become more specific in terms of their requirements for pitch,
rhythm and articulation, though it was still common for performers to apply embellishments and diminutions to the notated
scores; during the Classical Period a greater range of notational
specificity was introduced for dynamics and accentuation. All of
these developments reflected an increasing internationalisation of
music-making, with composers and performers travelling more
widely around Europe, whilst developments in printing technology and its efficiency enabled scores to be more widely distributed
throughout the continent. This process necessitated a greater
degree of notational clarity, as performers could no longer be
relied upon to be cognisant of the performance conventions in the
locality in which a work was conceived and/or first performed.

With Beethoven comes a new conception of the role of the
composer, less a servant composing to occasion at the behest of his

feudal masters, more a freelance entrepreneur following his own desires and convictions, and writing works designed as much for posterity as immediate accessibility and success. This conception bequeaths us the notion of the master-work, which is considered to exist as an autonomous entity over and above its various manifestations in performance, at least to a greater extent than hitherto, and which speaks to us universally, transcending the horizons of the era in which it was created[1]. An even greater degree of notational exactitude is required of such a work, with a view to performances in not just a different locality but also a different historical moment. One obvious manifestation of this is found in indications of tempo, where generic Italianate conventions are both rendered in the composer's native language and finely nuanced by qualifying clauses and adjectives. Through the course of the nineteenth century, tempo modifications are also entered more frequently into scores, and with the advent of a greater emphasis on timbre, scores gradually become more specific in terms of the precise details of instrumentation.

As the score came to be treated more reverentially, performers phased out the use of embellishment and ornamentation. In the twentieth century, this process was extended much further, with the finest nuances of inflection, rubato and rhythmic modification receiving precise indication in the score. By the time of the music of Brian Ferneyhough, to take one of the most extreme examples, all the most minute details of every parameter are etched into the notation, and the performer's task is simply to try and execute these as precisely as he or she can (the furthest extension of Igor Stravinsky's ideal of the performer as executor rather than interpreter[2], an attitude that is widely adhered to by performers of contemporary music).

Now, there is of course much truth in this narrative, or else it would surely never have attained the degree of acceptance that it

---

1. See Lydia Goehr, *The Imaginary Museum of Musical Works,* Oxford 1992, for more on this type of 'work concept'. The view of Beethoven I present here is highly indebted to that of Theodor Adorno, as presented in the posthumously collected *Beethoven: The Philosophy of Music,* translated Edmund Jephcott, Cambridge 1998.
2. See Igor Stravinsky, 'The Performance of Music', in *Poetics of Music: In the Form of Six Lessons,* translated Arthur Knodel and Ingolf Dahl, with a preface by George Seferis, Cambridge, MA 1970, pp. 121–135.

has, at least in some quarters. But in some ways it remains simplistic and dogmatically teleological. Whilst I do not write from the position of an expert in the performance of early music, I am keenly aware that the extent to which performers in early times freely improvised and embellished, or simply adhered to fixed conventions that may have been no less rigid than those which in later centuries would have been written, is at the very least ambiguous Such issues remain debated at least up until the Classical Period and also beyond; the degree of freedom which was available to or expected of performers varied significantly, depending upon whose music they played[3]. The nineteenth century saw parallel and opposing tendencies, with the simultaneous cultivation of both the 'star' composer and the 'star' performer, each of whom demanded their own degree of autonomous freedom from the other[4]. It is by no means conclusively established whether late-nineteenth or early-twentieth century performers necessarily took fewer liberties with the score than their early-nineteenth century counterparts[5], nor for that matter whether commonality of this type, delineated according to particular historical periods, is more

---

3. For example, Chopin in general was relatively strict with students concerning the performance of his own music (see Jean-Jacques Eigeldinger, *Chopin: Pianist and Teacher as seen by his Pupils*, edited Roy Howat, translated Naomi Shohet, with Krysia Osostowicz and Roy Howat, Cambridge 1986, in particular pp. 11–13, whereas Liszt, at least during his early 'virtuoso' period, was known for taking major liberties with the printed text (see Alan Walker, *Franz Liszt: The Virtuoso Years 1811–1847*, London 1983, pp. 316–318), and told his student Valérie Boissier in 1832 that he did 'not approve of polishing pieces meticulously', that 'Passions must be impetuous', and that 'One should express only what one feels' (see John Rink, 'Liszt and the Boissiers: Notes on a Musical Education', in *The Liszt Society Journal*, Vol. 31 (2006), p. 44). Boissier also noted his modifications to scores of Hummel and Weber (ibid. pp. 46, 52), and it may be possible to surmise from this and other evidence that he would not have been averse to other pianists taking some comparable liberties with his own music (I am not aware of any source from this period in his life in which he explicitly forbade or warned against such a thing).
4. For more on this subject, see Ian Pace, 'Instrumental Performance in the Nineteenth Century', in *The Cambridge History of Musical Performance*, ed. Colin Lawson and Robin Stowell, Cambridge, forthcoming.
5. Robert Philip, in his extensive investigation into early recordings, finds both areas of stylistic consistency and wild idiosyncrasies in approaches to vibrato, demonstrating if nothing else a plurality of approach in the early twentieth-century. See Philip, 'Tempo Rubato', in *Early Recordings and Musical Style*, Cambridge 1992, pp. 37–69.

striking than that which might be common to a region over a wider period of time.

But in many respects, it is the model of twentieth-century developments in both notation and composer-performer relationships that is the most inadequate[6]. Most obviously, developments in terms of notational detail have been paralleled by the exploration of graphic and other forms of indeterminate scores, and varying employments of performer choice and improvisation whose nature differs markedly from practices in earlier eras. I do not plan to deal with those types of works in this article; rather I wish to consider music with highly detailed notation to examine its relationship to performance and the possibilities it engenders.

## II.
## THE PERFORMER'S ENCOUNTER WITH
## NOTATION AS CRITICAL ALTERNATIVE

I first wish to offer an alternative model of musical notation itself which will inform much of the rest of the article. The whole historical construct I outlined above is, to my mind, founded upon an essentially *positivistic* view of the role of notation. By this I mean the notion that the score tells the performer in essence *what* to do, around which he can elaborate (through use of varying microdynamics, rubato, tempo modifications, etc.) depending upon the degree of notational exactitude. The alternative model I wish to propose draws upon structuralist thinking about language[7]; instead of

---

6. This conception seems intrinsic to much of the thinking about so-called 'modernist' performance as conceived in Richard Taruskin's *Text and Act*, Oxford 1995.
7. The literature on this subject is too vast to summarise here, but core texts are Ferdinand de Saussure, *Course in General Linguistics*, edited Charles Bally and Albert Sechehaye in collaboration with Albert Riedlinger, translated with introduction and notes Wade Baskin, New York, Toronto and London 1966, and Roman Jakobson and Morris Halle, *Fundamentals of Language*, fourth edition, The Hague 1980. A standard overview of the development of structuralist ideas is Jonathan Culler, *Structuralist Poetics: Structuralism, Linguistics and the Study of Literature*, London 1975. It is beyond the scope of this article to elaborate on the difference between structuralist and poststructuralist ideas; suffice to say that the conceptions I derive from the former are also informed by knowledge of the latter.

seeing the score in a *prescriptive* sense, telling the performer *what* to do, I would suggest that instead it delineates the range of possible performance activities by telling the performer what *not* to do.

Let me give a very simple example. A score indicates a group of three quavers played as a triplet. From a positivistic point of view, this would imply three notes each played for a duration of exactly one-third of a crotchet beat (that is literally *what* the score tells the player to do). Any deviation from this would represent some form of rubato. Now, in light of the fact that I believe that a metrically regular approach to triplets may be the exception rather than the rule in terms of historical (and even to some extent contemporary) practices, I find this sort of definition inadequate. Instead, this triplet should be viewed as being defined by what it *excludes*. There are a great many ways of playing the triplets in Example 1:

*Example 1. Chopin Impromptu in G-flat, Op. 51.*

Almost all of the melodic or accompanying figurations here are triplets, but they can be played with a variety of rhythmic inflections, reflecting other aspects of the melody, harmony and rhythm. A small tenuto can be placed at the beginning of the first and second bars to place some stress on the strongest beat and quasi-accentuate the dominant seventh harmony provided by the C-flat at the beginning of the second bar (as an alternative to the use of a regular accent, which might make the line unnecessarily jagged and also diminish the effect of the peak of the crescendo arriving between the second and third crotchet beats). The first notes on the first and third beats in the subsequent bars could be played similarly to enable a correspondence to be established between the melody and the two-crotchet duration groupings in the accompaniment. The more chromatic or dissonant melodic groups (for example the last crotchet of bar 2 and first crotchet of bar 3) could be expanded somewhat for added emphasis and 'breathing space'. Equally, the more diatonic or consonant groups (for example the second and fourth crotchets of bar 3) could be slightly accelerated. At the same time, the left hand figures could be played more regularly, leading to a de-synchronisation between the hands[8]. And, perhaps most crucially, the 'basic' triplet group could be played slightly unevenly (with the first note slightly longer than the other two, or perhaps more unusually, which the first and second shorter and the third marginally longer — of course there are many subtle variations of degree by which the performer can individuate their approach in this respect). All of these examples need not be considered as deviations but, instead, as some amongst the many possibilities for interpreting (in the sense of 'understanding') what the notational symbols used here can signify. However, if the basic pattern could be heard metrically as a semiquaver-quaver-semiquaver figure (which of course itself can be played in many different ways), then I would suggest that the performer is *not* playing triplets in any meaningful sense, as opposed to the above (and other) options.

So whilst in a sense it may be difficult to establish with any degree of certitude what a triplet *is*, we may be able identify what it is *not*. Similarly, there is an infinite number of different ways of playing *mezzoforte*, but a *mezzopiano* (let alone a *piano* or a *pianissimo*)such as would correspond closely to other occurrences of the latter symbol within the same piece or passage, would be strictly wrong — at least as the dominant dynamic for the passage marked as such. On discretely-pitched keyboard instruments, notation of

8. Numerous accounts of Chopin's playing and teaching emphasise his preferences in this respect: see Eigeldinger, *Chopin: Pianist and Teacher*, pp. 49–51,

pitch does indeed work in a positivistic sense (there is only one pitch that constitutes an A-flat within a particular octave, for example[9]). But on a stringed instrument, say, such a pitch could be played in various marginally different tunings, depending on factors such as the tuning system involved, whether the pitch is a leading note and thus to be sharpened or not, considerations of expressive intonation or other inflection relating to its harmonic function (or the tuning of other players with whom one is playing), and so on. So here an A-flat is not exactly a specific pitch, rather a range of possibilities that can be demarcated by considering what is excluded — an A natural, a G, or maybe an A-quarter-flat or three-quarters-flat as well, for example.

So, if a performer thinks of notation in this way, the task becomes less one of playing something 'right' as playing it 'not wrong' (which should not be taken to imply the relativist position that all 'not wrong' solutions are equally valid, only that they are not specifically excluded by the notation[10]). This may seem a contrived way of conceptualising notation, but it is one which I

---

9. However, whether this is notated as an A-flat or a G# can affect other aspects of how it is played, as I will explore later in this article in the context of the music of Morton Feldman.

10. The composer Howard Skempton has been known to remark in private that 'A piece of music is only as good as its worst performance' (my thanks to Mark R. Taylor for relaying this remark to me), by which I presume he means that 'worst' means 'worst but not excluded by the notation'. This is a very hard-line position to take on notation and interpretation (but one that seems particularly vivid and noteworthy in the context of Skempton's own often sparsely notated work) which I would not wish wholly to subscribe to. Skempton may have also been indirectly alluding to the problems Feldman encountered with his own early works involving indeterminate notation in this respect (Feldman commented that in his early graphic scores that the 'performers sounded bad ... because I was still involved with passages and continuity that allowed their presence to be felt' ('Autobiography', in Walter Zimmermann (ed), *Morton Feldman Essays*, Kerten 1985, p. 38, later published as 'Liner Notes', in B.H. Friedman (ed), *Give My Regards to Eighth Street: Collected Writings of Morton Feldman*, Cambridge, MA 2000, p. 6). It is also worth noting Feldman specifically refused permission for Cornelius Cardew to mount a performance of one of the *Projections* series using instruments different to those in the score ('Unpublished Writings', in Friedman (ed), *Give My Regards to Eighth Street*, pp. 206–207). This was one possibility that the score definitively excluded. Frank O'Hara's conceptualisation of how 'the performer must create the experience within the limits of the notation' in *Piece for Four Pianos* (1957), 'New Directions in Music: Morton Feldman', ibid. p. 215, corresponds very closely to the model of notation I am outlining).

believe has positive benefits in ways I hope to demonstrate in the context of contemporary music. I chose an example from Chopin deliberately because his music begs these questions as much as any from the standard piano repertoire. In reports of his playing of various mazurkas, for example, the three beats in a bar were so stylised that some believed it was written in four[11]. That might seem to reveal a weak point in my model of notation (according to which something in four would be strictly wrong[12]); but I believe, bearing in mind the poetic licence which may apply in such a report, that most sensitive listeners would nonetheless perceive the difference between a highly stylised mazurka rhythm performed in the manner described and something that is actually being played (and, more importantly, read) as if it is in a time signature of four.

# III.
## CONTEMPORARY MUSIC, NOTATION AND PERFORMANCE:
## AN ELLIOTT CARTER CASE STUDY

To look at what is at stake in the interpretation of notation in contemporary music, I should like to begin with a reasonably standard example, well-known to many pianists who play new music, Elliott Carter's short piece *90+* (1994). The work seems extremely precisely notated in terms of pitch, rhythm, dynamics, articulation, and so on. But there are nonetheless a huge number of questions which the performer must answer for him- or herself. Example 2 shows the opening of the piece.

For the first two lines or so, there is a continuous chordal progression, each chord consisting of three or four notes from a six-note chord. Around this, in his characteristic fashion, Carter pre-

---

11. As remarked by Sir Charles Hallé, who said that Chopin's performances of his Mazurkas 'appeared to be written, not in 3/4, but in 4/4 time, the result of his dwelling so much longer on the first note in the bar' (Eigeldinger, *Chopin: Pianist and Teacher*. p. 72).
12. It should be borne in mind that this is a very particular idiomatic use of rhythm for which an expanded concept of what 'three in a bar' means may be required.

*Example 2. Elliott Carter, 90+.*

sents various types of 'punctuation' which first take the form of single pitches from the same six-note chord at varying dynamics and articulations. Then, with the introduction of the G-flat and D at the end of bar 6, the pitch gamut widens; furthermore, in bar 4 the hairpin dynamics indicate that the 'punctuation' pitches begin to form into lines. The tempo direction consists solely of a metronome mark, crotchet = 96, with no other expressive indication. As this marking will, on the next page, undergo a metrical modulation to crotchet = 120, one can fairly assume that, at least when that modulation approaches, the original tempo is to be maintained in some fashion. But in the intervening bars, is the pulse to be kept quite strict, or is there room for some local deviation for 'expressive' purposes? I will demonstrate in a moment examples of how some might wish to do this, but first let us examine other basic questions that arise from the very outset.

The opening chord consists of four pitches all marked *piano*. But how is one to voice this? If one plays all the notes literally at the same dynamic, there will be a slight imbalance as the lower notes sound stronger — this aspect becomes more pronounced in more widely-spaced chords. Followers of certain schools of playing might wish to 'top voice' the chord slightly; whilst there is nothing in the score specifically to indicate this, there is nothing to forbid it either. Bearing in mind that Carter frequently works with performers trained at American music colleges, where the top-voicing, all-purpose *cantabile*, approach is sometimes standard practice[13] (especially amongst those who have studied with expatriate Russian teachers or within the schools they bequeathed), he would presumably be aware of this. However, later, in bar 37, Carter writes '*bring out upper line, cantando*' in a passage of a similar nature; from this we can fairly assume that the later passage is thus to be differentiated from the opening (or else he would surely have written such an indication there as well).

If one plays the chord with a very subtle voicing so that each note is very slightly louder as one goes from bottom to top, it is possible to create an *audible* equality between the pitches, rather than a *literal* one as mentioned before. None of these possibilities is necessarily 'right', in the sense of implying others are 'wrong', but nor is any of them clearly 'wrong' according to the notation. There are other possibilities as well; one might wish to bring out the presence of an E-flat triad within the opening chord by playing the F slightly softer than the other pitches. This could make the 'contradiction' of the tonality provided by the following E-natural more pronounced, if that is what one wishes. And other distinct voicings designed to foreground certain harmonic properties of later chords are equally possible. Peter Hill writes of how Messiaen was enthusiastic about the many possibilities in this respect in the *Catalogue d'Oiseaux*[14], in which questions of voicing are even more complicated by virtue of the presence of various

---

13. This convention has sometimes invoked the wrath of composers, notably Debussy, who according to Marguerite Long said 'The fifth finger of virtuosi, what a pest it is!' (Long, *At the Piano with Debussy*, translated Olive Senior-Ellis, London 1972, p. 13). See also note 14 for Messiaen's similar sentiments.

dynamics within chords, which can themselves be interpreted in a variety of ways; the issue is further exacerbated by the dynamically complex chords in the first two of Stockhausen's *Klavierstücke*[15]. So, let us now consider the dynamics and articulation of the 'punctuation'. The first note in the bass, E-natural, is indicated *mf*, *with* an accent and a tenuto marking. Leaving other dynamics to one side for a moment, consider how one interprets and executes this accent. It might be seen to imply that the note is slightly louder than the basic level one determines to be *mf*, or it might be read as to imply a certain sort of attack. I would play the B-flat and G with the second and third fingers, and then use a slight rotary throwing motion on the fifth[16] to aid the approach on the E, absorbing the reaction from the key with a certain resilience in the joints and wrist. For reasons which are beyond the scope of this article to explicate in depth, such a mode of touch, from a clear distance above the key, will produce a degree of 'key noise' (the sound of the finger striking the key), which merges to the ear with the sound produced by the hammer hitting the string, so as to give a slightly sharper-edged beginning to the note[17]. But this is only one possibility; the E could be played from closer to the key so as to minimise the possibility of such key noise; once again, those of certain schools of playing would frequently favour such

---

14. See Peter Hill, 'Messiaen on his own music', in Hill (ed), *The Messiaen Companion*, London 1995, pp. 275–277. Hill also points out that Messiaen 'detested the gratuitous bringing-out of the top note' (p. 275).

15. In Ronald Stevenson's *Western Music: an introduction*, New York 1971, a book which exhibits that combination of scepticism towards modernism and neo-romantic idealisation of 'world music' that is a common feature of a certain school of British musical discourse, he argues that one of these chords, with four different dynamics in one hand, is 'simply unplayable by a human hand, whether the person attached to it is called Smith or Horowitz' (p. 188) and goes on to suggest that this was what led Stockhausen to electronics. However, numerous performers (for example Aloys Kontarsky, David Tudor, Herbert Henck, Bernard Wambach or Ellen Corver) have clearly disproved Stevenson's claim.

16. By this I mean a motion whereby the forearm rotates on its axis in the direction of the held notes, so as to provide extra distance from which the finger(s) can be thrown towards the keys. This is a technique derived from the method provided in György Sándor, *On Piano Playing*, New York 1982.

17. To those who would deny that 'key noise' is ever audible, I would recommend listening to Sylvano Bussotti's *Pour Clavier* (1961), which includes a (highly audible) section played mostly just on the surface of the keys.

an approach, as a note with a sharper-edged attack is often considered by them to be harsh and unacceptable. Then there is the question of how the note is to be released; I could raise the finger briskly from the key (after holding it for its full duration) with a further rotary motion, causing the damper to fall rapidly and produce an abrupt end to the note. Alternatively, I could slow the release of the finger, and thus cause the damper to hit the string less abruptly, by the use of an upward wrist motion whilst releasing.

The right-hand B-natural is marked staccato and *mezzo piano*. Again I can use a throwing motion to play this if I so desire or play from closer to the key followed by a quick release (this approach would however be likely to be somewhat less abrupt than that produced by the 'bounce-back' of the throwing motion).

These are all, of course, minute details, but in combination can quite significantly affect the nature of the audible result and how it might be perceived. The question of attack for the punctuation (or, for that matter for the chords, for which similar questions arise), is especially important: the extent to which one differentiates the two groups of attacks (for punctuation and chords) will affect the extent to which the different layers of musical information are perceived as being stratified.

At the risk of over-generalisation, I would argue that a less-stratified approach accords more closely with many interpretative aesthetics associated with those who concentrate primarily on the standard repertoire and come from relatively traditional and well-established schools of teaching[18], whereas the more-stratified one might be seen as a more 'modernist' approach. This is not at this stage to imply any dogmatic value judgement as regards these different approaches (and all the other possibilities), though I do observe that the former seems very much more in fashion at the time of writing. I will return to this point later.

Carter indicates in the score that the pedal is to be used solely to join one chord to another. But this can be done in different ways,

---

18. At least in the twentieth century; there is ample evidence to suggest quite different approaches to this were common in the nineteenth, especially in certain French, Germanic and Hungarian schools of piano playing, though this is too large a subject to investigate in the context of this article.

depending on the exact point at which it is released, and the manner of doing so. A quick release exactly on the attack of the new chord causes a clear progression in which the chords are connected, indeed seamlessly, but form a line in an essentially accumulative manner. A slower release, or a release very marginally after the attack, blurs the overlap somewhat, creating a sense of a particular manifestation of line as something over and above the simple sequence, even as a type of 'aura' which further exacerbates the difference from the punctuation[19].

When the punctuations start to form themselves into lines, there are various ways in which one can use small tempo modifications to heighten this feature if so desired. The end of bar 4 contains a written out *accelerando*, but a slightly quickening of the pulse *on top of this* might make the relationship sound less obviously 'metrical' or mechanistic. Similar principles could also be applied in bars 6 and 7

The passage at the end of bar 7 and beginning of bar 8 could be played as if the E-flat is an appoggiatura, thus helping to consolidate a sense of a temporary tonality of B-flat in the left hand. This can be done by playing the E-flat slightly louder than the notes on either side of it, whilst maintaining a basic dynamic of *mezzo forte*. In order to further heighten this sense of tonality, one could play the B-flat slightly later than indicated, and the D slightly earlier, so as to marginally compress the figure.

These are just some of the various decisions for performers, even in these eight bars alone (I have not talked about, for example, how one gauges both absolute and relative dynamics, which is another important issue). If one tried to rethink these questions anew with every single note, it is unlikely the piece could be played without spending a huge amount of time learning just a single page (this may be a desirable option, but hardly practical at least for performers of contemporary music, who are generally expected to continually learn and maintain a very large repertoire). Many performers

---

19. Charles Rosen points out that Moritz Rosenthal told him that this type of 'syncopated' pedalling was purely a product of the nineteenth century, though Rosen himself doubts this (Rosen, *Piano Notes*, New York 2002, p. 210). See also Kenneth Hamilton, *After the Golden Age: Romantic Pianism and Modern Performance*, Oxford 2008, pp. 170–174, for more on the issue (Hamilton is more sceptical about Rosenthal's claims and suggests various possible motivations for them).

will have simply established a set of conventions for themselves with respect to these aspects of performance practice, which they apply across a range of distinct repertoire; this consistency plays an important part of the construction of a unified performing style that can be promoted and marketed as part of their commodified personalities. Whilst a performer needs to make decisions, even if temporary ones, and get on with the business playing the piece (furthermore, a spontaneous approach to such parameters in live performance can be most fruitful), it is still worth his while to be aware both of the range of choices available, how many different ways there are of playing 'what is written', and perhaps most importantly what the result of different approaches entail in a wider context.

A reasonably competent pianist could at this stage attempt to play these three lines: if one plays the passage first adopting the above-mentioned parameters so as to stress continuity, integration between parts and lines, and organic development, then the same passage with an emphasis upon stratification of simultaneous lines, sharp delineation of characterisation, and non-integration of successive sounds, including in a temporal sense, one should hear almost caricatured versions of what might be called a conventionally 'musical' interpretation in the first and a mannered form of modernist alienation in the second.

If one knows the recordings of Carter string quartets by the Juilliard Quartet on one hand, and the Arditti Quartet on the other[20], one might recognise how these approaches are mirrored to an extent in the playing of either group. If my own preferences lie closer to the latter than the former, this is not least because of a profound scepticism to what I might call the 'jargon of the natural'. The first approach grounds the music in familiar (and institutionalised, though not necessarily historical) performance practices in the wider classical music world, whereas the latter (which can in extreme form become equally reified) stresses the non-identity and

---

20. The Juilliard Quartet have recorded the Carter Quartets several times, the recording I have in mind hear is that from 1991 of the String Quartets Nos. 1–4 and Duo for Violin & Piano, on Sony Classical S2K 47229; for the Arditti Quartet I have in mind the two discs containing the String Quartets Nos. 1–4 and Elegy, on ETCETERA KTC 1065 & 1066.

non-assimilability of the piece entirely within such practices and the musical aesthetics they imply. Above all, the latter at best stresses those things which make the piece *unique*, how it exceeds the boundaries of any previous models (of course this quality is denied if it is assimilated into an equally anonymous mannered 'modernist style', though I believe the latter can potentially offer a wider range of possibilities). And that approach makes a positive virtue out of Carter's subjective individuation of the composing process, in contradistinction to a subjugation of his work within a more normative and anonymous field of practices. The ideological implications of such distinct approaches should be clear; these are very pressing concerns in the field of contemporary music performance at the time of writing, and are connected with the construction of Carter as the *eminence grise* of new music, made acceptable when his music can be made to sound sufficiently 'old', firmly located within an idealised organic world that is presumed to constitute the past.

## IV.
## MAURICIO KAGEL'S ANTI-IDIOMS

I now wish to consider a very different example, where the notation serves to *defamiliarise* musical material that might otherwise

*Example 3. Mauricio Kagel,* Passé Composé.

imply a certain idiomatic approach. The passage in Example 3 is from Mauricio Kagel's extended piano piece *Passé Composé* (1993).

*Example 4. Kagel, melody from* Passé Composé, *bars 63–67, a possible phrasing based upon the inherent melodic properties of the line.*

This passage, from bar 63 onwards, uses a notational strategy common in many of Kagel's later works[21]. Were the dynamics, phrasing and articulation left free, one might be inclined to play the melody line somewhat like in Example 4:

The phrasing and voicing in this manner (one of several possibilities) gently reinforces the contours of the melody; one might also balance the E-flats and D-flats in the bass (playing the former generally softer than the latter), so as to clearly imply a tonal centre of C# or D-flat minor. Whilst to some extent this latter key is indeed implied by the writing, there is no unequivocal resolution because of the particular dynamics and phrasing. In various senses, Kagel's dynamics in particular are quite radically counter-intuitive; for example, the final semiquaver of bar 65 is marked at a higher dynamic than the two notes on strong beats which surround it. The balance of voicing between the hands is also in a continual state of flux, neither ever clearly assuming the role of a *Hauptstimme*.

---

21. Without the dynamic markings, this would be what Kagel elsewhere refers to (in the context of a passage from the stage work *La Trahison Orale/Der Mündliche Verrat*, which also occurs in the Piano Trio) as a 'seamless winding melody' (*pausenlos windende Melodie*—'.../1991: Ein Gespräch zwischen Mauricio Kagel und Werner Klüppelholz', in Klüppelholz (ed), *Kagel ...*/1991, Cologne 1991, p. 51). Many of Kagel's later works feature melodies constructed from quite banal figurations, including descending diatonic, modal and chromatic scales. See Björn Heile, *The Music of Mauricio Kagel*, Aldershot 2006, esp. pp. 140-141, for more on this.

But this is not simply a type of belligerently anti-idiomatic writing on Kagel's part, 'different' for difference's sake. The first two-and-a-half bars in the right hand roughly correspond to what one might 'naturally' play; what alters things is the presence of the left simultaneously, whose dynamics serve to gradually reinforce (though never in a thoroughly affirmative manner) the sense of a D-flat pedal point, which on the third system of the page is revealed to be a dominant of G-flat. The right hand then seems to react to the ways through which its very identity is disoriented by the left, so that the final semiquaver of bar 65 sounds like an attempt to 'compete' with the latter, then 'corrected' with the next note which balances the voices. After this the right hand gains confidence, building to a sustained *forte*. This sort of highly distinctive interplay could only be achieved by such counter-intuitive notation as Kagel uses. There are numerous other comparable examples throughout the piece and elsewhere in his output.

When once rehearsing Kagel's *Piano Trio* with two string players, I remember comments from them about how Kagel supposedly did not understand how to write for their instruments, as the bowings they encountered seemed so unidiomatic. Despite my own expressed sentiments to the contrary, I was unable to persuade them not to rewrite them. By so doing, they were writing out a fundamental aspect of Kagel's music — the very fact of composing 'against the idiom' in order to forge extremely individuated modes of expression that run contrary to habitual expectations. Yet their very strangeness, at least at first, unfortunately tends to count against performers in the eyes (or rather ears) of many critics.

This process of 'performer recomposition' is common; during one student rehearsal session in London, the performers had similarly changed Kagel's markings in favour of something supposedly more idiomatic to the instruments. In rehearsal, he insisted that they did what he asked; alas, after the performance, I remember one critic in particular bemoaning the fact that the phrasing and articulation sounded 'unnatural', or words to that effect, blaming the performers for this. Such a critic, I believe, was looking for a musical expression that offered the comfort of the familiar; Kagel's music, and the forms of negation he employs though notation, work precisely to counteract such things.

# V.
## PIERRE BOULEZ, NOTATION AND RECORDED PERFORMANCE

Let us look at an example which raises the issue of how one interprets notated beaming, and the implications in terms of metre.

*Example 5. Pierre Boulez, Second Sonata for Piano, from second movement.*

In this movement, a passage of rather complex counterpoint, built from manipulation and development of small cells, 'clarifies' in Example 5, as the music approaches a climax (arrived at via a long-range crescendo), by the use of regular periodic units in each hand: quavers in the right, dotted semiquavers in the left, so as to produce a 3:4 ratio. In the recording of the piece made by Maurizio Pollini[22], I hear what amounts to a simple 3/8 metre (or 6/8, possibly); the music could have been notated in two parts with simple beaming in groups of three and four notes in either hand[23], as in Example 6.

Actually the right hand in Boulez's notation consists entirely of staggered groups of four quavers as indicated by the beaming[24]; similarly the left hand consists of groups of four dotted semiqua-

---

22. Originally recorded in 1976, the pressing I refer to is on a CD together with works of Stravinsky, Prokofiev, and Webern, Deutsche Grammophon 419 202-2.
23. Charles Rosen comments on how Boulez employs a technique derived from Messiaen by which barlines appear to contain an extra beat, so as to avoid their signifying rhythmic regularity. See Rosen, 'The piano music', in William Glock (ed), *Pierre Boulez: A Symposium*, London 1986, p. 92.

*Example 6. Re-notation of passage in Example 5.*

vers. This notational configuration acts as a negation of the wholly regular pulse that would result from the version I wrote out, and which I hear in Pollini's performance. It demands some imagination from the performer to clarify this defamiliarisation of what would otherwise be a regular pattern (and would as such serve an overly cathartic function in the context of what is otherwise a high degree of metrical irregularity). One way to do this is to put a slight stress on the first of each beamed group of four, and play the last of such groups a little less than the other notes, combined with an ultra-legato touch in both hands to emphasise the connectedness of notes within a group.

But there is the further question of how to 'think' the pulse. By this I mean the designation of the metrical unit the performer thinks of as the pulse, playing the other part relative to this [just trying to avoid ending a sentence with a preposition]. The easiest possibility in this case is for the pianist to think in quavers; this is what I believe Pollini does, and which is clearly implied by Boulez's indication of '*reprendre un peu en dessous de la nuance*'. The passage clearly echoes a slightly earlier passage (Example 7) in which there are regular semiquavers in one hand combined with

---

24. On Boulez's wider use of four-note periodic cells in this sonata (especially in the first and last movements), see Thomas Bösche, 'Zu Deuxième Sonate (1946–1948) von Pierre Boulez', in Orm Finnendahl (ed.), *kontexte: Beiträge zur zeitgenössischen Musik. 01. Die Anfänge der seriellen Musik*, Berlin 1999, pp. 37–96 (especially pp. 76–78, 84–87) and more briefly in Gerald Bennett, 'The early works', in Glock (ed), *Pierre Boulez: A Symposium*, pp. 77–81.

triplet quavers in the other (also with beaming in staggered groups of four in each hand). Here it is easier for the pianist to think in terms of semiquavers or quavers as the basic pulse, though no clear reason why one should not equally think in terms of triplets. In either case, I have found that one's choices create audible hierarchies, but one should ask: why this is the case? One reason might be because of the by-product of a certain small, unconscious stylisation of whichever group is *not* the thought pulse, which is thus played somewhat less metrically rigidly.

*Example 7. Boulez, Second Sonata, from second movement.*

# VI.
## MORTON FELDMAN AND NOTATIONAL 'SPELLING'

In Morton Feldman's extended piano piece *For Bunita Marcus* (1985), the 'spelling' of the notation (in the sense of the choice of accidentals) indicates a variety of things that are worth considering. The piece is notated at a single dynamic (*ppp*) throughout, with a pedal indication at the beginning and otherwise just two places where he marks no pedal for identical mini-flourishes, after which the pedal is retaken. There are also no slurs or articulation markings. In terms of how exactly to play the work within the notated dynamic, in terms of subtle nuances and so on, we have only the beaming, barring, bar grouping with respect to repeats, and spelling to go on, combined with apprehension of other musical properties of the work. Most of the piece is taken up by interactions and dialogues between several categories of material, mostly consisting of just a few pitches which are permuted, rhythmically modified, shifted by the octave, or occasionally subject to pitch development. A passage roughly in the middle of the work makes much of a group of three pitches, C# an augmented octave above middle C, the E above that, the D# above that, and a high F a diminished 10th above that, always notated as a grace note. The minor third formed by the simultaneous resonance of the two lowest pitches clearly implies a C# minor tonality, the high F reinforcing this by acting somewhat in the manner of an appoggiatura. The passage in Example 8 starts from well within the reiteration and permutation of this pitch cell.

Feldman returns to another cell based upon F#, C#, D and E, which has already been extensively developed earlier in the piece, like a fading memory, before returning to the other pitch cell. But at the top of page 37, he does something remarkable, producing a moment quite unlike anything elsewhere in the piece. He sharpens the E to an E#, and lowers the high F to the A# below, thus creating a sense of modulation into the tonic major. This is very short-lived, as Feldman flattens the E# back to an E after this has been repeated once, then makes matters more murky by flattening the C# to a B#, and reintroducing the A#, so that the combination of E# and B# can be seen to resolve chromatically onto E and C#, giving the earlier seeming modulation into the major a retrospective context.

In light of what I am describing in terms of the harmonic progress (unusual within the piece because of the use of pitch development), one should consider the notation at the top of page 37. The large 2/2 silent bar in the middle of the group blurs any perceptible temporal relationship between the two bars containing notes; with the pedal depressed, they sound almost identical in

*Example 8. Morton Feldman,* For Bunita Marcus, *pp. 36–37.*

terms of pulse (making the first bar with notes in the following group between repeat signs more striking for its rhythmic contrast). As the first E# heralds a quasi-modulation, should it be stressed very slightly, as one might do with a comparable process in a more traditional work? Or should one just let it emerge without any such heralding? Perhaps neither of these options is preferable, on account of the particular grouping of bars. This depends upon whether one interprets the use of repeated groups as being merely a notational convenience, or whether it signifies something of greater musical consequence. I am inclined towards the latter explanation for the following reasons: both of the two preceding groups of bars (as delineated by repeat signs) begin with a C# followed by a D#, a quaver apart, as does this one. As such the other pairs of notes in each group might be interpreted as an extension and enrichment of the sonority, and might be played very marginally quieter, as 'weak bars' compared to the 'strong bars' at the beginning of the groups. Then the tonic major modulation can sound quite different, growing out of such enrichments, rather than necessarily heralding a major harmonic shift, and in this manner attaining a more melancholy than affirmative character.

The pitch cell most extensively used in the piece consists initially of A-flat below middle C, G a major seventh above, C above that, and B-flat above that, notated as two temporally staggered, arpeggiated dyads in either hand, as can be seen on page 31, second system, third bar (Example 9).

*Example 9. Feldman,* For Bunita Marcus, *p. 31, second system.*

This comes almost immediately after the second mini-flourish, which thus serves to herald the introduction of such material. Soon afterwards, all pitches are shifted up a semitone, and this becomes the basic unit. Example 10 gives one example of how this pitch cell is reiterated and temporally permuted.

*Example 10. Feldman,* For Bunita Marcus, *from pp. 45–46.*

I first got to know this work well from a recording which I owned for two years before I purchased a score. This material had always sounded like an axis of relative tonal stability, establishing the dominant key as that of A major, combining a minor seventh in the right hand with a major seventh in the left. And if I had transcribed the work from my recording, I would have notated it as A, G#, C# and B. But this is not how Feldman notates it; the intervals he presents are an augmented sixth in the right hand and a diminished octave in the left. If this were written for strings, it would be possible to make this clear by different tunings, but no such option exists on the piano. How to try and make Feldman's particular spellings manifest in sound is a major challenge in this piece. After both performing it myself and hearing it played by others, I have come to believe that a certain unconscious tendency to think of this cell as being 'in A major' implies a certain type of voicing, in which the A and D-flat are very slightly more prominent than the B or A-flat. But this 'A major' feel can be somewhat deferred by a different approach, entailing the playing of the D-flat and A-flat at a very even dynamic so as to stress the interval of a perfect fourth. If the D-flat is slightly more than the B, then it is less likely to imply the interval of a minor seventh. But at the same time, the barring should be taken into account, over and above what might seem a 'natural' harmonic voicing. If the beginnings of each bar are stressed very slightly, the tonality is defamiliarised even more. At the same time, the pairs of pitches in the left hand can be played with the first A very slightly louder than the A-flat, so they sound like a dyad. This would thus make the low A the strongest pitch, followed by the A-flat and D-flat (both played equally), with the B the quietest; the latter modified in line with the barring.

This is of course one of various possible solutions; whichever one chooses, it is important to bear in mind and act upon the counter-intuitive notation, working *against* the assimilation of this music into a notion of 'tradition' (in terms of particular forms of tonally-derived models of tension and release), even if this makes the music less amenable to what might be called a 'chill-out' form of listening, a manner of appropriation I fear is all too frequent in Feldman performance today.

# VIII.
# MICHAEL FINNISSY PRO AND CONTRA TRADITION

Many works by Michael Finnissy explicitly allude to different 'traditions', and as such raise the question of the relationships between Finnissy's pieces and their sources in performance. The first of these I would like to consider is from his first book of *Gershwin Arrangements* (1975–88), his setting of 'They're writing songs of love, but not for me'.

*Example 11. Michael Finnissy, 'They're writing songs of love, but not for me', from* Gershwin Arrangements.

Finnissy has a continually developing figuration in quavers in the left hand (itself an allusion to Liszt's *La Lugubre Gondola I*[25]). In the second, fourth and some later bars, he adds a dot to the first

---

25. Finnissy would later return to this work in the chapter *My Parents' Generation thought War meant something* from his epic piano cycle *The History of Photography in Sound*, though here it is combined with a Soviet War Song. Finnissy pointed out to me the link between these two pieces (both preoccupied with death) alluding to the same Liszt piece.

quaver. Now, the means of interpreting this has always fascinated me. When I first asked him about the piece, I wondered if this was simply shorthand for a certain expressive holding back at these points, a slightly vague way of using notation in order to tell the performer to do precisely that. He said that this certainly was a notated rubato, but was precisely *that* rubato in the score. Now, thinking about the notation in this manner can significantly affect the result. If seen as a vague indication of a holding back, the natural tendency would be to slightly anticipate the dotted quaver with a minute elongation of the previous quaver, and do the same with the quaver that follows the dotted one, so as to ease smoothly into the expansion and back out again. Similarly, on the third system, the extra quaver rest at the end of the bar (breaking with the general pattern of groups of three quavers), could be interpreted simply as a comma or 'breath', and similarly anticipated by a small ritardando in the preceding group.

But this is not what I believe Finnissy intends. If the basic quaver pulse is kept reasonably steady (except where the *poco accel* is marked) then the dots, tempo modifications and rest produce a markedly different form of psychological expression. Instead of *expansions* of the pulse, the dots become *interruptions*, like heartbeats that are only half the length they should be. The *poco accel*, and the tuplet group before the rest, if also played in such a context of an otherwise steady pulse, become moments of a certain nervous tension as the pulse is compressed, anticipated by the close chromatic harmony in the third bar of the third system. Then the rest becomes a momentary void, after which the music begins to 'try again', thus defamiliarising the cadence into G major.

This approach accords much less with a received 'musicality', but produces a more striking psychological complexity even within such a short passage, and to my mind, is integral to the work's modernity, presenting fragmented and unstable consciousness as an alternative to nostalgic refuge within models of organic wholeness. But one's decisions in this respect may reflect what type of piece one believes this to be, or more broadly, one's sense of Finnissy's cultural significance. Is this music a slightly more chromatic neo-tonal homage to an archaic idiom, or rather an attempt to reconfigure such an idiom in a manner that is wholly contemporary, or simply deeply personalised? The former may be likely to win more plaudits from certain critics for whom something called 'modernism' is essentially a dirty word and once again value music of the present to the extent to which it can be situated within the realms of that which they already know and with which they feel comfortable[26].

This issue is even more acute with the fifth piece in Book 1 of Finnissy's *Verdi Transcriptions* (1972–2005) (Example 12). This work has caused me no end of interpretive grief, and to this day I remain somewhat undecided on how best to play it. Finnissy takes the melody from the Septet with Chorus 'Vedi come il buon veglardo...' from Part 1 of Verdi's *Ernani*, set in such a way that makes necessary (for simple practical reasons) a reading with tempos significantly slower than are common for performances of the Verdi original. He configures this with a certain degree of added chromatic harmony[27], though to such a degree as to subvert the clear tonality. However, the right hand consists of a two part atonal, very free, canon, seemingly independent of the left.

Finnissy clearly marks the hands *equilibrato*, and has often insisted on this to me, yet how to make this audibly meaningful in performance is by no means easy. The 'identity' of the left hand is much more obviously distinctive because of its tonal harmonic progression, whilst the right hand has no clear sense of linear direction. When simply played literally 'equally', the left hand still tends to occupy the foreground (also because it is in a stronger register; other comparable Finnissy pieces including others in the revised and expanded Verdi cycle, in which the tonal material is

---

26. I suspect that this type of attitude has informed certain attempts to construct Finnissy primarily within a late-romantic pianistic tradition (which is undoubtedly a major influence) and play down ways in which his work might resonate with modernistic forms of fragmentation, discontinuity and defamiliarisation. For more on the construction of an anti-modernist critical aesthetic of performance in general, see Ian Pace, 'Verbal Discourse as Aesthetic Arbitrator', in Björn Heile (ed), *The Legacy of Modernism*, Aldershot 2008.

27. As if a (mild) allusion to one of Leopold Godowsky's works for left hand, as Finnissy also does in various other works, notably the fourth of his *Yvaroperas*. See Ian Pace, 'The Piano Music', in Henrietta Brougham, Christopher Fox and Ian Pace (eds), *Uncommon Ground: The Piano Music of Michael Finnissy*, Aldershot 1998, [pages — will confirm] for more on this.

*Example 12. Michael Finnissy, 'Vedi come il buon vegliardo…', from* Verdi Transcriptions.

placed in the right hand, sound quite different in this respect). It is very easy to subdue those right hand notes which cause greatest dissonances with the bass, thus rendering them as passing notes and further consolidating the bass tonality; this heightens the cathartic function of this movement, in a way that all other pieces in this book seem to be heard relative to this one, acting in totality like a magnified 'tonal centre'.

In performances of this type (including some of my own in earlier years), I have heard listeners almost always identifying this piece as their personal favourite (save for a few hard-line avant-gardists who react negatively); I am confident that this is the result of its large amount of tonal material, more comforting either than Finnissy's more extensively mediated by-products, or than material so far removed from the original as to seem almost wholly new (such as the right hand, which in some distant sense is itself derived from the Verdi melody). To try and get away from encouraging this conception, I attempted various strategies. One was to accentuate the most dissonant notes in the right hand so as to attempt to destabilise the bass, but this approach seemed over-didactic. I realised better results could be achieved by thinking of the right hand as much in terms of rhythm and metre as pitch. So I would slightly accentuate the beginnings of beamed groups in the right hand (as suggested earlier in the context of Boulez), play them with a high degree of rhythmic exactitude, and make particularly clear those moments when the pulse shifts through tuplet groupings, rather than aiming for a more mellifluous approach. This would thus create a stronger sense of rhythmic presence, marked by discontinuities or at least shifts in pulse, enabling a more pronounced sense of the treble as a pair of *lines*, rather than merely a constellation of pitches forming an essentially decorative function around the central melody.

## IX.
## COMPLEX MATTERS: KARLHEINZ STOCKHAUSEN AND BRIAN FERNEYHOUGH AND THE LEARNING EXPERIENCE

In my final two examples, I wish to look not only at the aesthetics of performance, especially with respect to duration, metre and rhythm, but also at what might be entailed in one's approach to the learning process itself. To put it another way, I want to consider not just what one *does* in performance, but also how one arrives at the situation which makes such things possible. The two things are linked and have deeper implications than might be realised, as I hope to demonstrate.

Much relatively 'complex' modern music (or indeed music of earlier eras as well) contains a large degree of information in terms of the range of possibilities that are directly implied by the score; no less significant are other knowledge and perspectives performers bring to bear upon it, concerning performance practice and conventions, perceptions regarding the a piece's nature, its relationships both to other music (including that which may accompany it in a programme) and a wider cultural sphere, the degree of audience familiarity (which of course depends on the audiences in question) and the real-time interaction between the performer and the audience at the moment of performance. The totality of all this information is more than any performer could possibly consciously control at all levels during a live performance. On the most basic level, one learns pitches, rhythms, dynamics, phrasing, articulation, tempo, tempo modifications, and so on, but can rarely devote equal attention to all of these when actually performing. For this reason, the performer engages in a process of *prioritisation*, both when learning the work and when performing it.

In a work with highly intricate notated information with respect to these parameters, one often learns it by concentrating upon different aspects of the music at different stages in the learning experience. This becomes an issue from the very first moment one takes a piece to the instrument. One might begin by loosely playing through the piece, paying less attention at first to the fine details whilst trying to gain some conception of the whole. In the process of learning, one then tries to focus in on the details and refine them, without losing sight of one's initial overall conception, though being prepared to modify this in light of what is learned during that process of small-scale focusing. Alternatively, one might begin by working on small details, refining these as best as one can before moving onto other passages, gradually building up speed, and so on.

These are the two extremes, and their very possibility is to some extent conditioned by such factors as the performer's ability to sight-read[28]. They parallel what I have elsewhere[29] described as 'top down' and 'bottom up' approaches to composition: in the former case, the composer begins by working out the architectural and global aspects of a composition, then hones in on the details; in the latter case, he starts with small cells or gestures and develop these into a piece, deriving the architecture from these low-level materials' own immanent properties and implications. Both of

---

28. Though, conversely, one's ability to sight read might be heightened by awareness of the possibility of the former approach.
29. See Ian Pace, 'The Panorama of Michael Finnissy (I)', in *Tempo* No. 196 (April 1996), p. 25.

these positions are of course vast simplifications; most composers simultaneously employ some degree of both; the potentially antagonistic consequences of their co-existence in the compositional process can serve to energise the whole work. There are few more disappointing pieces than those which seem to consist of a reasonably well-judged overall structure, but in which the small-scale material is little other than 'filling', or conversely those works that pedantically develop their material aimlessly, their composer never seeming to stand back and consider the macroscopic properties of the work, its architecture or drama.

This dichotomy can also be applied to performance. Many performers employ a combination of the two approaches when learning a piece. Nonetheless, I do not intend to infer from this that some 'happy medium' is the optimum way to learn any work; rather the particular degrees of emphasis, as manifested on various levels, are crucial in enabling one to learn the works at all, and should continually be re-evaluated when approaching each new work. Furthermore, the very sequence of learning, and the priorities applied during the different stages, affect and reflect both one's own perception of the work (itself sometimes in a state of relative flux) and how it is likely to be perceived by listeners.

A piece which raises these issues is Stockhausen's *Klavierstuck X* (1954-55, rev. 1961). This work of a little over twenty minute's duration has become notorious as a result of several of its attributes. One is the use of glissandi in clusters, necessitating the pianist's wearing of fingerless gloves to diminish friction with the keys in the process of so doing (though alternative approaches have been tried, using talcum powder on the keys and so on). Another is the highly virtuosic and volatile continuous passage at the very beginning of the work, which is then set into relief for the remainder by virtue of the separation of passages with silences. Stockhausen composed it using a sophisticated system (detailed amply in Herbert Henck's book on

---

30. Herbert Henck, *Karlheinz Stockhausen's Klavierstück X: A Contribution Toward Understanding Serial Technique*, second edition, translated Deborah Richards, Cologne 1980. For the most perceptive and well-researched work on of Stockhausen's early compositional aesthetics and techniques, including within the *Klavierstücke*, see Christoph von Blumröder, *Die Grundlegung der Musik Karlheinz Stockhausens*, Stuttgart 1993.

the work[30]), involving post-serial techniques of permutation for various parameters, so as to create a particular type of distribution of a range of fragments, between which there are a plethora of multi-layered correspondences achieved through other highly developed compositional techniques. On the most basic level, I hear the work as opening with a sharply characterised 'cosmic explosion' (itself with a high degree of inner variegation) which recedes a little so as to allow greater apprehension of the various categories of fragments (or atomic dust, if one likes) that emerge out of such an explosion. At least, that is my overall perception, derived first from hearing the work played by others, then modified and nuanced on the basis of learning and then performing (and re-learning) it on repeated occasions. Others might find different aspects of the work of greater interest, which will affect how they approach both learning and performing it. To be more specific, Stockhausen's use of pitch (including the pitches at which cluster glissandi both begin and end) is carefully controlled, generally exhibiting types of serially-informed distributions that mostly eschew anything with too obvious tonal implications or other forms of directional harmony (there are a few passages which are exceptions to this), including in those short sections which limit themselves to a restricted gamut of pitches. This necessitates care that one does not inadvertently play such wrong notes as might produce unwanted directional harmonic implications, but perhaps does not require such a high degree of attention to every pitch as would be required in a tonally or post-tonally organised work. Dynamics, on the other hand, are extremely carefully gauged, variable (but

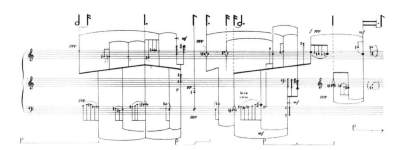

*Example 13. Karlheinz Stockhausen,* Klavierstück X, *p. 13, second system.*

not to such an extent as produce a totally decentred experience of dynamics, as might be said of a work such as *Kreuzspiel*, in which every note in the piano has a different dynamic), and are intrinsic to articulating the drama of the work. In many passages, one encounters lines of pitches which form linear sub-strata of wider textures, indicated and manifested through the use of dynamics. One of these would be the passage on the second system of page 13 (Example 13). In this case such an effect is also produced by the contrast between grace notes and more sustained durations.

If one looks at the succeeding fragment on the top system of page 14, it can be seen to grow out of the pitches made to sustain at the end of the preceding passage, with the addition of a low B. Something akin to a conventionally lyrical line emerges out of a more diffuse and aperiodic texture.

But Stockhausen's scheme for notating duration (and thus, by implication, metre and rhythm) demands the closest attention in the context of this article, as well as in my opinion in the conception of the work as a whole. The score is divided piecemeal into consecutive short segments, notated continuously, each of which is assigned a duration relative to a basic unit. This is indicated through the use of standard durational units, quavers, crotchets, minims, etc. Every passage demarcated by such units is to be fitted into such a duration, relative to a basic pulse which is 'as fast as possible'. This takes some work on the part of the performer to execute satisfactorily, not least because the spatial distribution of the score by no means necessarily corresponds to the intended durations. If one looks, for example, at the second system of page 2 (Example 14), from the notated minim underneath the instruction about cluster glissandi onwards, one sees one group of units (beginning with a cluster glissandi starting at G–C) to be played within the duration of a minim, then another group within the duration of a semibreve tied to a quaver i.e. a total duration of nine quavers. However, the amount of horizontal space assigned to this latter group is somewhat less than two-and-a-quarter times that of the previous group (two-and-a-quarter being the ratio between the two durations). The sloping beams in the second group indicate free accelerandi and ritardandi (for upwards and downwards slopes respectively). The first group contains six equal units, which I thus play roughly as quaver triplets; the second group contains fifteen unequal units. The mean duration of these would thus be a unit of 9/15 quavers, so 3/5 of a quaver, very marginally less than 2/3, which is the duration of a triplet quaver. The first units in the group need to start at a slower pace than this mean unit; yet, they are notated considerably closer together than those in the preceding group. If one also looks at the second group as a whole, one will see that the downward slope of the beam incorporates a few more chords than the upward one, suggesting a slightly longer duration to be employed on this downward slope, which can if one chooses be used to achieve a certain rhetorical effect as the group approaches its conclusion (this effect is also produced by the particular dynamics and pitches employed).

*Example 14. Stockhausen,* Klavierstück X, *p. 2, second system.*

This particular approach to notating duration has various consequences. Perhaps the most significant of these is that which differentiates it from, say, Stockhausen's earlier *Klavierstuck VI*, in which Stockhausen notates a sliding scale of pulse throughout (though this was a late addition to the score for publication[31]). That notational scheme, as with most of the other earlier *Klavierstücke*, derives duration, metre and rhythm in terms of a continually shift-

31. I am grateful to Pascal Decroupet for pointing this out to me. See also Decroupet, 'First sketches of reality. Fragmente zu Stockhausen («Klavierstück VI»), in Finnendahl (ed), *Die Anfänge der seriellen Musik*, pp. 97-133, on Stockhausen's use of tempo and rhythm in this work and its different versions.

ing *pulse*, even where this is not directly played (in the sense of there being periodic notes). In those pieces, the performer is presumably intended to think through the work, both when practising and performing it, in terms of these shifting pulses which are indicated through metronome marks. *Klavierstuck X* is quite different; there is a singular pulse from which one conceives time units, *within* which groups are to be accommodated. A somewhat crude way of describing the distinction would be to say simply that the earlier pieces are predicated upon metre, and this is predicated upon duration. If I say that in *Klavierstuck X* pulse is for the most part merely a highly localised affair, compared to the earlier works, I do not simply mean that the latter contain more explicitly articulated pulses compared to this (actually in some ways the reverse may be true), but that in terms of the psychological consequences of the notation, pulse may become less central to the performer's experience when playing it. Of course the caveat must be that this depends on the particular strategies employed for learning and performing it; nonetheless, I believe this distinction to hold true.

This view perhaps reflects certain ideologies I bring to bear upon the work, which entail their own consequences, one of which I will try and demonstrate now. The passage on the top system of page 3 (Example 15) is highly demanding from a pianistic point of view.

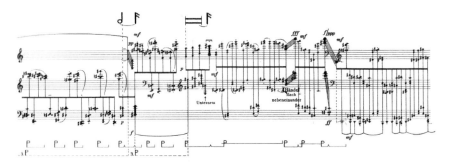

*Example 15. Stockhausen* Klavierstück X, *p. 3, first system.*

In the group below the minim tied to a semiquaver, there are continuously shifting chords in quick succession; the same is true of the groups that succeed it. By virtue of the notated durations, several of the groups of individual chords come to have a duration of approximately a triplet semiquaver. This I conceive not so much in terms of a pulse as an estimation of the duration with which to start each group, allowing for some degree of flexibility for practical or other reasons. However, at the basic overall pulse that I choose for the work, these passages are likely to sound somewhat frantic, hurried, and may lose some clarity in the process. By virtue of the particular set of priorities I bring to bear upon the piece, I decided that this effect, including the slight loss of clarity, is one with which I am happy when it enables me to maintain the sense of drama that results from the rapid tempo. That decision itself results from other convictions concerning the relative importance of pitch, articulation, clarity of gesture, and so on. In the process of practising or re-practising this, I play these things slowly and with a certain fastidious attention to pitch accuracy on some occasions, to evenness of duration at others, or to clear distinctions between articulations or dynamics at others. At other times, my attention is directed more to the totality of the groups or their interrelationships, and to maintaining the speed; because of my own individual prioritisation, these aspects of the music are more at the forefront of my mind when performing it. For other parameters, to some extent the practice hopefully 'does its work'. My choice of prioritisation of *psychological focus* when performing in concert has further implications: it enables a degree of spontaneous interaction with respect to these aspects of music at that very moment of performance, which is less possible with other aspects. And for that reason, that spontaneous focus almost certainly manifests itself in a hierarchy of *projection* at that time.

Henck advocates that the performer should create his own tape loops with verbal countings of durations that delineate each group[32]. The performer can then practise the piece with these to ensure the durations are accurate. I considered doing this, but ultimately decided against it after finding that it was possible (with a reasonable amount of experience of learning very complex rhythmic patterns in other music) to attain the durations simply by counting; by this strategy I felt that, psychologically, the possibility of being able to maintain some intelligent sense of flexibility

---

32. Henck, *Stockhausen's Klavierstück X*, pp. 63–64.

was more immediate, rather than feeling a little oppressed by the ominous sound of this click track haunting me even when it is not actually present. A click track, like a metronome, is inhuman in the sense that it derives from the process of exact and simple calculations, wholly avoiding the minute intricacies or even personal vulnerabilities that would in some sense inform a human attempt to produce or think such durations oneself, whether from a conductor, following another player, or simply counting to oneself. It is for this reason I prefer the latter option, which leaves open the option of some degree of interaction between the counting and one's response to the actual material being played.

What I have just suggested about an ongoing interrelationship between counting and responding to the demands of the material could easily be misinterpreted: some could take it to mean that simply one should play 'what the material demands in and of itself' and adapt the mental counting around that. That perspective assumes an organic relationship between the durations and the material which I do not believe to be appropriate in this piece; rather, the durations sometimes constitute an external, inorganic imposition upon the material. To give another example of this: if one looks at the second system on page 29, there is a series of chords grouped by beamings, to be accommodated within a duration of a semibreve tied to a quaver i.e. a total duration of nine quavers. At a basic quaver pulse of somewhere between 96 and 120, these chords are relatively slow, indeed much slower than I have otherwise heard.

Now, some might feel that the chords, especially in terms of their resemblance to other passages or general material in the piece, imply a somewhat quicker duration. Within such a context, this reading might seem more 'natural' or familiar, regardless of the actual duration Stockhausen writes, and the slower tempo sounds contrived. But I believe that a performer should at least consider the possibilities that a more contrived result could have been desired, intended, or at least allowed, or that there may be other way of creating musical sense out of such defamiliarised material.

The response of some to the raising of such questions might be to invoke the old cliché of the 'spirit' versus the 'letter' of the

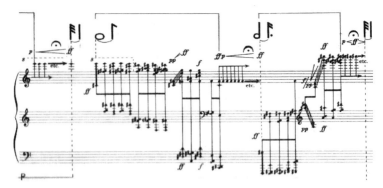

*Example 16. Stockhausen* Klavierstück X, *p. 29, part of second system.*

text[33]. But this is a false dichotomy: how one conceives the 'spirit' affects how one interprets the 'letter', and conversely how one interprets the 'letter' affects how the 'spirit' is perceived, either by oneself or by a listener. The process of learning and performance entails a continuous two-way interaction between these poles, each one frequently modifying the other. In the case of the passage in Example 16, one's perception of the 'spirit', entailing a certain set of priorities, might suggest a particular tempo, possibly a quicker one. But conversely, one should be equally open to the possibility that close investigation of the letter of the text, specifically in this case the notated duration, might modify one's perception of the spirit of this particular passage and its relationship to the rest of the work. The text is not simply something to accommodate within one's *a priori* conception of 'what type of piece this is' (or, more broadly, 'what type of composer Stockhausen is' or even 'what music should be in general' It is surely fruitful to allow such a conception to be informed and nuanced, even perhaps significantly altered, both by one's close study of the details of the text, and other wider self-reflexive considerations concerning one's reasons for arriving at such *a priori* conceptions in the first place. And this parallels the processes that are experienced by many composers who begin work on a piece with a certain generalised conception of what they intend, but as they work in more detail upon

---

33. In recent times, this dichotomy is invoked strongly by Richard Taruskin, in 'The Limits of Authenticity', in *Text and Act*, pp. 75–77.

both micro- and macroscopic elements, discover these to have immanent implications that exceed the boundaries of such an initial conception, which becomes enriched as a result.

My final example is the opening of Ferneyhough's piano piece *Opus Contra Naturam* (1999–2000), which I premiered. The first bar of the piece (Example 17) contains startlingly complex rhythms, with three or even four levels of nested tuplets.

*Example 17. Brian Ferneyhough,* Opux Contra Naturam, *opening.*

An immediately obvious immediate question is 'can these rhythms possibly be played accurately?' I believe this is the wrong question; rather we should ask 'why has Ferneyhough notated them in this manner?' It would be disingenuous to deny that there is any redundancy whatsoever in Ferneyhough's notation from a performer's point of view. Indeed, he has made clear that the score for him represents something of an ideal rather than simply a specific set of instructions[34]; some of these may be the result of particular compositional procedures that could be notated differently or more simply with little perceptible difference in terms of the audible result, though I believe this situation to be very much the exception rather than the rule.

With the 'structuralist' model of notation that I mentioned at the beginning of this article in mind, we should look at this first bar as a means of channelling the performer away from what might be more habitual or familiar modes of interpretation. Take, for example, the first group: relative to the basic metronome mark

---

34. For Ferneyhough's most extensive thoughts on notation, see 'Interview with Philippe Albèra', in James Boros and Richard Toop (eds.), Time is Time: Temporal Signification in Music.

of quaver = 54, we have first an 11:7 tuplet. An 11:7 quaver at this tempo would be at a rate of approximately MM 84.9. A further 5:3 modification produces MM 141.4, so a semiquaver within such a group would be at MM c. 283. Thus a group of three semiquavers has a total duration of a single pulse at about MM 94.3. That provides duration for this group and a 3:2 relationship with the group that follows. Now, within this first group, there is a further 5:3, modified by yet another around the second to sixth semiquavers. At this point, now that I have such a duration, I can execute a group of notes which in their total duration end a little before the duration is over, thus providing the rest, and at which the second to sixth notes are at an accelerated pace. This pace is not quite as fast as a doubling of the pulse would be, however (that would be a 6:3 relationship). Whether I would play this rhythm 'accurately' is perhaps not the point; I may not know if it is exactly 'right' in the sense of how a computer would play it, but I can detect certain results that are definitely wrong. It would be wrong if I played the group entirely evenly, if the second to sixth notes existed in a 2:1 metrical ratio to the first, or if the group took so long that the rest was imperceptible. And the durational relationships between the different groups can be gauged in a similar manner. Here I am employing a combination of both positivistic and structuralist approaches to interpreting the notation, which in this situation I find most fruitful, positivistic in the sense of calculating the metronomic durations down to the second level of nested tuplet, structuralist after then.

Some of Ferneyhough's markings may be the result of strict application of compositional procedures, some more intuitively applied. Whichever, this approach is the result of a conviction, based in part on what Ferneyhough has written about his conception of notation, that the detailed markings are a way of negating habit, a way of creating figures that exceed the boundaries of the 'already heard', quite simply a 'cultural' rather than 'natural' approach to compositional production. All composers, except for the wholly derivative, do this to some extent, Ferneyhough simply more radically than most. Perhaps this should be considered in light of the fact that Ferneyhough does indeed employ a gestural vocabulary that frequently has clear late Romantic or Expressionist connotations, thus making more urgent the necessity of individuation.

Now, I could not think about all these things when actually performing the bar. But in the process of learning it, I try to pay attention to these aspects, especially the need to avoid slipping into habit, until the results become 'second nature' when I can confidently execute them when relaxing a bit more, and thus pay more attention to other aspects of the music. It is from *that* perspective that it then becomes possible to introduce some other freedoms in the execution without hopefully reverting back to habit.

In many of the examples I have discussed, the aesthetic ideals I am aiming for resist the 'organic'; rather, they stress discontinuity, tension between co-existing parts that are not necessarily made to blend seamlessly, and above all, defamiliarisation. These ideals and their concomitant strategies can easily turn into a fetish of their own, becoming mannered and indeed 'familiar', thus negating their original function. I have certainly fallen into this trap myself on some occasions. Interpretative strategies need to be continually re-examined when learning a new piece or re-learning an old one. But at heart they represent a strategy of *resistance* in performance; resistance towards certain ideological assumptions that entail absorption of musical works into the culture industry. This absorption itself entails a harmonisation of the antinomic elements within such works, the smoothing out of such discontinuities as can produce psychological estrangement or simply cause fragmentations and incompleteness within the musical experience such as demands some active input from the listener if their listening experiences are to become coherent. If these are not papered over, then the musical work repudiates passive listening, much more so than when it is presented as an organic and hermetically-sealed whole. This type of musical aesthetic, whereby musical works exist in a critical and dialectical relationship to wider experiences and consciousness (and by implication to the world), is to my mind one of the most important ways in which music can become more than passive entertainment. Looking hard at the relationship between notation, metre and time, is one of the most powerful ways of enacting this in practice.

# PERSONALIA

## MARK DELAERE

MARK DELAERE studied musicology and philosophy at the K.U.Leuven and music theory, harmony, counterpoint, clarinet and chamber music at the Royal Conservatories of Music in Antwerp and Brussels. He received his Ph.D. in musicology in 1988, upon which he became research fellow at TU Berlin from 1989 until 1991 (Humboldt-Forschungsstipendium). In 1992, he was appointed Associate Professor and in 1995 full professor at the K.U.Leuven's musicology department. He founded MATRIX, a new music education and documentation centre with one of the most extensive collections of contemporary music scores. Mark Delaere's research covers music from the 20th and 21st centuries, with a special focus on the interaction of analytical, historical, theoretical and aesthetical methodologies. He has published eight books, and is currently preparing a volume on early serialism for *Analysis in Context. Leuven Studies in Musicology.*

## JUSTIN LONDON

JUSTIN LONDON is Professor of Music at Carleton College in Northfield, MN, where he teaches courses in Music Theory, The Philosophy of Music, Music Perception and Cognition, and American Popular Music. He received his B.M. degree in Classical Guitar and his M.M. degree in Music Theory from the Cincinnati College-Conservatory of Music, and he holds a Ph.D. in Music History and Theory from the University of Pennsylvania, where he worked with Leonard Meyer. His research interests include rhythm and meter, music perception and cognition, the history of the Delta blues, and musical aesthetics. He is the author of several articles in the recent revision of the revised *New Grove Dictionary of Music* and the *Cambridge History of Western Music Theory.* His book *Hearing in Time* (Oxford University Press, 2004) is a cross-cultural exploration of the perception and cognition of musical metre. He served as President of the Society for Music Theory in 2007–2009.

## PASCAL DECROUPET

PASCAL DECROUPET studied music and musicology at the Royal Conservatory of Music and the University of Liège and later in Berlin, Paris and Basel (Paul Sacher Stiftung). He was a Research Fellow at Humbold Universität in Berlin in 1994–1996 and taught at the University of Liège. In 1996–2001, he was Director of the Centre de Recherches et de Formations Musicales de Wallonie (studio for electronic music). Since 2005, he has been Professor at the University of Nice Sophia-Antipolis. Publications on contemporary music include the edition of writings by Henri Pousseur and the edition of the sketches and manuscripts of Pierre Boulez' *Le Marteau sans maître*.

## BRUCE BRUBAKER

Pianist BRUCE BRUBAKER studied at the Juilliard School, where he was awarded the school's highest prize (Edward Steuermann Prize, 1983). He earned three degrees at Juilliard: Bachelor of Music (1982), Master of Music (1983) and Doctor of Musical Arts (1992). He joined the undergraduate faculty at Juilliard in 1995 and in 2001, he joined the school's graduate faculty and created an interdisciplinary performance course bringing together musicians, actors and dancers. In 2004, Bruce Brubaker was named to the piano faculty of Boston's New England Conservatory. In 2005, he became Chair of the conservatory's piano department. Bruce Brubaker's discography includes 'glass cage', 'inner cities' and 'Hope Street Tunnel Blues', including music by Philip Glass, John Cage and Alvin Curran (on Arabesque). Following his debut at Lincoln Centre's Alice Tully Hall, Musical America named Bruce Brubaker a Young Musician of the Year (1988). Brubaker has premiered music by John Cage (Seven), Mark-Anthony Turnage (Entranced), Jonathan Lloyd (Won't It Ever Be Morning) and performed Glass's piano music in concerts and broadcasts throughout the world. Brubaker has appeared with the Los Angeles Philharmonic, New York's Orchestra of St. Luke's, as part of the St. Louis Symphony's Copland 2000 Festival, at Leipzig's Gewandhaus, Lincoln Centre's Mostly Mozart Festival, the Hollywood Bowl, at Tanglewood, Antwerp's Queen Elizabeth Hall and at Finland's Kuhmo Festival. In November 2005, Brubaker performed in Carnegie Hall's tribute to composer Meredith Monk at Zankel Hall in New York.

## IAN PACE

Pianist IAN PACE was born in Hartlepool, England in 1968 and studied at Chetham's School of Music, The Queen's College, Oxford and, as a Fulbright Scholar, at the Juilliard School in New York, where he studied with the Hungarian pianist György Sándor. Based in London since 1993, he has pursued an active international career, performing throughout Britain, Europe and the US. Playing a vast repertoire, with a particular focus on 20th and 21st century music, he has given over 150 world premieres, played in 22 countries, and recorded over 20 CDs. Amongst the composers whose work he has premiered are Julian Anderson, Richard Barrett, James Clarke, James Dillon, Pascal Dusapin, Brian Ferneyhough, Michael Finnissy, Christopher Fox, Volker Heyn, Hilda Paredes, Horatiu Radulescu, Frederic Rzewski, Howard Skempton, Gerhard Stäbler and Walter Zimmermann. He has played as a concerto soloist with the Orchestre de Paris (with whom he premiered the piano concerto of Dusapin), the SWR Orchestra in Stuttgart and the Dortmund Philharmonic amongst others, and has appeared at most of the major new music festivals. He has given cycles featuring the piano works of Stockhausen, Kagel, Lachenmann, Ferneyhough, Radulescu, Finnissy (whose complete piano works he performed in a landmark six-concert series in 1996, and whose five-and-a-half hour *The History of Photography in Sound* he premiered in 2001), Rihm, Skempton and Fox. He is also a writer, musicologist and teacher: he taught at the London College of Music and Media from 1998 to 2001, was an AHRC Creative and Performing Arts Research Fellow at the University of Southampton from 2003 to 2006, and in 2007 took up a position as Lecturer in Contemporary Musicologies at Dartington College of Arts; he has also taught piano at Festival Acanthes in Metz, and Impuls in Graz, as well as giving many guest lectures and masterclasses. His musicological work focuses upon 19th and 20th century performance, issues of music and society, and in particular the post-1945 avant garde. His *Brahms Performance Practice: Documentary, Analytic and Interpretive Approaches* will be published by Ashgate in 2010; he is also currently writing a chapter on 19th century instrumental performance for the forthcoming *Cambridge History of Musical Performance* and researching into the social and political context of the first generation of avant-garde composers in West Germany.

## DARLA CRISPIN

Dr. DARLA CRISPIN is Senior Research Fellow in Creative Practice of the team of Research Fellows within the Orpheus Research Centre in Music (ORCiM) and at the Royal College of Music. Her research concentrates upon performance and philosophy in musical modernism and post-modernism, with particular emphasis on the Second Viennese School.

EDITORS
Darla Crispin
Kathleen Snyers

SERIES EDITOR
Peter Dejans

AUTHORS
Mark Delaere
Justin London
Pascal Decroupet
Bruce Brubaker
Ian Pace

LAY-OUT
Wilfrieda Paessens, Ghent

PRESS
Grafikon, Oostkamp
Bioset, 100gr

ISBN 978 90 5867 735 8
D/2009/1869/20
NUR 663
© 2009 by Leuven University Press /
Universitaire Pers Leuven / Presses Universitaires de Louvain
Minderbroedersstraat 4, B–3000 Leuven (Belgium)